THE BLESSINGS AND CURSE OF MIDLIFE

KRISSY REGAN
THE WELLNESS POET

First published by The Wellness Poet in 2024
Copyright © 2024 Krissy Regan
ISBN

Paperback - 978-0-6489348-9-9
eBook - 978-1-7637734-0-0

Krissy Regan has asserted her right under the Copyright, Designs and Patents Act 1988 to be identified as the author of this work. The information in this book is based on the author's experiences and opinions. The publisher specifically disclaims responsibility for any adverse consequences, which may result from use of the information contained herein. Permission to use information has been sought by the author. Any breaches will be rectified in further editions of the book.

All rights reserved. No part of this publication may be reproduced, stored in or introduced into a retrieval system, or transmitted in any form, or by any means (electronic, mechanical, photocopying, recording or otherwise) without the prior written permission of the author. Any person who does any unauthorised act in relation to this publication may be liable to criminal prosecution and civil claims for damages. Enquiries should be made through the publisher.

Cover design: Krissy Regan, The Wellness Poet
Layout and typesetting: Krissy Regan, The Wellness Poet
Editor: Cathy Joyce

Krissy's Disclaimer

This book was not written using the help of AI or ChatGPT. And I'm darn proud of that...

The contents and themes of this book are designed to entertain and inspire you. Please do consult a professional therapist or doctor if you need help AND contact any of the readily available support services in your community if you are feeling depressed, suicidal or just need a safe space to vent.

The views shared in this book are largely my own and no deliberate misrepresentation of the views and work of others is intended.

Acknowledgements

I could not have written this book without the support of my friend and editor Cathy Joyce. There is an expression which says: *There is no breakthrough without a breakdown.* And, good writers write what they know! What I know right now is that midlife is full of obstacles, blessings, and sadly some curses. As our skin loses its elasticity, and our resilience starts to fade we must recognise and acknowledge that mid-life has arrived, and we can and should reflect on the skills and abilities we have accumulated that will help shape our future. We can also decide to be a new person in the future and figure out who that person wants to become.

Thanks to my other amazing contributors who shared their stories with us. Antoniya Beyriyska, Edd Shoebridge, Anthony Mak,

Andrea Diniz and Louise Vangestel. I'm sure you will find their stories relevant and relatable, if not to yourself then to someone else you know.

I would also like to thank Glasbergen Cartoon Service for allowing me to use 8 of their amazing cartoons in this book. I chose ones I hope will make you smile and reflect the themes shared throughout the book.

Contents

Introduction 1

Chapter 1: Recognising Midlife 5

Chapter 2: Midlife Moments from Around the World 17

Chapter 3: Health in Midlife 33

Chapter 4: Wealth in Midlife 53

Chapter 5: Work in Midlife 67

Chapter 6: Dealing with Death 87

Chapter 7: Midlife Masterclass 109

Afterword: Midlife and Then What? 129

About the Author 137

Introduction

How are YOU doing?

If you are reading this book, you might recognise yourself in the middle of your life and at a stage where your life experiences, and your self-awareness are causing you to question everything.

A lot of useful education and literature exists about childhood, adolescence, and the elderly and very little is written about the middle stages of life. I would argue that this stage of life is even more confronting than the others because you are old enough and hopefully still healthy enough to realise that the only person that can navigate you through this is YOU!

As a society we are living longer so technically speaking midlife starts later than, say, for our parents' generation. But let's presume you may tap out in your 90s, then 40-50 is quite likely the mid of your life... Now, don't get depressed: This is both an exciting time and a time for reflection and change.

The general curve of life for the average person tends to flow in the following way.

0-19 – school, parents, growing up, having fun, feeling powerless and possibly bullied, rebelling, moving out, worrying about stupid crap.

The Blessings and Curse of Midlife

20-30 – finding a job, figuring out how to live with strangers, experiencing workplace politics and bullying colleagues, partying a bit, experimenting with drugs, credit and sex, and practising being a grown up while having fun.

30-40 – settling down, accessing more credit, not getting as much sex, having kids, figuring out playground politics and school bullying, working and generally having less fun.

40-50 – worrying about too much credit and why your sex organs are letting you down, saying *f-you* to workplace bullies, getting rid of people and stuff that has no value to you, and thinking of ways to bring fun back into your life.

Does this sound familiar for you?

In the following chapters we will explore Health; Wealth; Work and Dealing with Death. I've reached out to some people around the world who have insights and experience with these challenging topics. It's been a blessing to write this book at a time in my life where I'm contemplating what my next 49-years may look and feel like. On turning 49 I realised I have overcome all the curses that have been gifted to me, and I've had to learn many new skills to move forward to the future that I want to create. In an age of information, it's easier to learn, grow and overcome our inherited stuff. I hope this book helps people reflect on some of their stuff, and to visualise a future that is healthy, fulfilling, and empowering.

Introduction

I wanted this book to be small enough to read in an afternoon so that you can then read it a few times over. I like plain-speak, honest, wholistic ideas backed by other renowned people you may or may not have heard of yet. Do check them out and you could find your brain changing as it's scientifically proven that when we learn new things, do new things, and go to new places we create new pathways in our brain. Also drink lots of water as our brain needs water to function. Dehydration causes brain disfunction.

Grab a glass of water and let's get learning!

My notes and reflections

Chapter 1
Recognising Midlife

The Blessings and Curse of Midlife

When you turned 30 did you think, "Oh My God, I'm 30," and you suddenly felt old and wise: like somehow surviving your 20s and being 30 was a huge achievement? When I turned 30, I remember telling people I was OLD now.

I DO NOT want to sound disrespectful to any of my 30-year-old readers, however, what I would say to you is that you 'ain't quite there yet' so keep the youthful exuberance, all night energy, and ambition as long as you can my friends.

At 49, when I tell people I'm middle-aged they try to dismiss my grumblings.

"YOU ARE NOT MIDDLE-AGED."

"AHhh, YES, I AM!"

I can do math; I know the average age of death, for women in my country: I know that I am indeed "midlife". And I am proud of it. I'm not going to pretend that I'm not middle-aged.

OK, I do still colour my grey roots, I haven't been brave enough to grow-out to grey yet. I'm not into sticking needles in my face, so I will happily allow wrinkles to take over my face and at some stage I will give up the bottle (hair dye) and let my hair do its natural thing.

I love midlife. I love being a mature-aged mum of young kids who allow me to be silly and share special times doing the things they love. I guess I came to fully recognise and embrace midlife by the

Recognising Midlife

age of 45. I was in the midst of a lot of change in my life, a lot of questioning, and a lot of reflection on some challenges faced by my older friends.

I was adventurous as a teen up until my thirties, and after two children at aged 39 and 42, I became vastly less adventurous in some areas of my life. I realised that midlife adulting was extremely challenging and I was in a constant state of sacrifice and believe me at times I felt very resentful. I had compromised away my health, wellbeing, time and career to have a family and I was not regretful, but I was not exactly brimming with joy about how to juggle this stage of my life. Something had to shift. So, I had a full-blown midlife crisis and that was when I firmly acknowledged I had arrived at midlife.

A midlife crisis, by its very design, is both a blessing and curse as it forces you to revaluate all areas of your life. It's usually a time that any unresolved trauma rises to meet you head on, often at the worst possible time and with no warning. So, the scenario for many women goes something like this: old-fashioned dating advert in the newspaper.

> *Middle-aged woman woke up this morning and is looking for a new direction. Her boobs have shrunk, her hips are wonky from carrying her kids and her career has stalled while she has been sleepless for the past 5 years. She is very kind, intelligent and hardworking and would just like to be respected and paid fairly for the work she does every day. She still has a lot to offer*

The Blessings and Curse of Midlife

when the kids are not home sick, and she will answer calls in the middle of the night any day of the week. She doesn't waste money on getting her nails done anymore but she would like an hour to herself once a week to feel like a normal person. When she is not busy with her own children, she is helping her parents or her friends. She is a very appreciative person, and can multitask, and find lost socks with her eyes closed. She still has ambition but would like her ambitions to be matched by the right supports at work and home for her to achieve her full potential, attend all the school activities, and be an active member of her community... AND if at all possible, she would like to pursue a hobby. Thank you!

This book is not going to dwell on the typical midlife crisis symptoms but if you are in the midst of your life and you are noticing some changes in the way you think and feel about everything then chances are you may be "entering" or "in" your midlife crisis.

A midlife crisis may occur anytime from the ages of 35 to 65. Individuals can adopt simple strategies to cope with the symptoms of a midlife crisis. The simplest are increasing physical activity, talking with others, and changing how they think about aging.

Increasing your level of physical activity may bring a natural boost to your mood as well as your overall health and vitality. However, feelings of shame and isolation are common symptoms of a midlife crisis because it's often hard to articulate what you are really

Recognising Midlife

feeling. A downturn in happiness during middle age is a relatively common experience and research indicates that happiness levels are generally at their lowest at the age of 47. Rather than ruminating on the past or dreading the future, developing a new mindset is important to face the future with empowerment and agency. Getting older is rife with possibilities, and new experiences.

I would direct you to a helpful article on the symptoms of a midlife crisis and you can consider some ways to get support. https://www.forbes.com/health/mind/midlife-crisis/

The curse of a midlife crisis is that often it will come during other significant milestones (or events) in your life such as a middle-age health issue/crisis, caring for elderly relatives while raising your own family, taking on more debt to get a bigger house or car, dealing with the loss of loved ones, career change, teenagers, relationship breakdowns, or other uncontrollable disasters.

If you started a family in your 20s it's possible you may become an empty nester whilst dealing with a midlife crisis, increasing your feelings of loneliness, loss of purpose, and isolation.

My advice to friends, colleagues and clients is to embrace your midlife crisis.

1. Recognise the overwhelming uncertainty and embrace the changes ahead.
2. Re-evaluate your purpose.

3. Remember your hobbies.
4. Focus on your health and wellbeing.
5. Instead of thinking about aging, think about what you will do in the second half of your life with all the accumulated knowledge, the experiences and connections you now have.

And remember - All of this is NORMAL!

I like to joke that I've now entered phase 3 of my midlife crisis.

Phase 1 – moved my family from England back home to Australia aged 43.

Phase 2 – wrote 5 books and ran 3 marathons aged 45-48.

Phase 3 – downsized house to simplify life and wrote book 6 (this book) and ran 2 more marathons taking me to age 50!

I do feel my midlife crises have been healthy and life-affirming. I did all the unhealthy stuff in my 20s and 30s. I quit a few jobs during different phases of my midlife crisis as I just couldn't seem to get back to the highs of my career before I became and a mum, and I became unhappy with the hidden pressures of being a working mum with two small children. I say hidden pressures, but all mums know what I'm talking about: childcare costs; lost time with children; commuting time; household chores; family admin and not enough leave entitlement to cover all the school holidays and pupil free days adding to stresses and pressures at home and work.

I will talk more about Work in Midlife in Chapter 5.

Let us consider how our traumas may jump up to bite us in our midlife. Those who may have experienced childhood trauma or those that have experienced narcissistic abuse, sexual abuse, or other forms of abuse will generally start to feel its impact as their youthful resilience starts to wane. My unscientific explanation for this is simple.

In our 40s our central nervous system has been under stress for many years. We may have experienced behavioural patterns and relationships that became unsustainable as we started to gain clarity and insight on who we truly are. The coping mechanisms we used to survive those unpleasant experiences start to fail us and anger, rage, resentment and sadness rise to meet us. As midlife adults we start to fully understand what behaviour is NOT acceptable and it's highly likely we want to keep our children safe, and we are trying to **break a cycle of abuse**. It's hard to break cycles of abuse unless you confront your own feelings, and as soon as you start to confront your feelings you can't hide from them any longer. Hence you must deal with your trauma.

Shame prevents us from speaking freely about our trauma, so we tend to keep it to ourselves. One of the great things about the internet is that there is so much information available now

The Blessings and Curse of Midlife

regarding all kinds of trauma and narcissistic abuse. If you are curious about your behaviour patterns, relationship choices, limiting self-beliefs, unhealthy habits such as emotional eating, smoking, drinking, shopping, hoarding etc. there is literally a world of useful information that could help you navigate how you deal with your trauma and overcome it.

I personally have found journaling, curiosity and self-reflection have helped me recognise, and acknowledge, the impact of trauma in my life and to develop healthy and constructive ways to process it. That is not to say I don't feel discarded, hurt or angry at times, but I can make sense of those feelings when they rise up and change my thoughts accordingly.

It's quite normal in midlife to wonder if we have enough money to retire. Our parents may have retired at 55 or 60. Money is a very personal thing and our attitude to money may dictate how we balance our desire for security versus enjoying life now. You never know when it will end right? We will talk about Wealth in Midlife in Chapter 4. What I would say now is that life is unpredictable, everchanging, and we are only here for a short time. What feels secure for one person may not feel secure for another. Our desire to save or spend could also be relative to our generational trauma and if we devote some time to understanding what security looks and feels like, and communicate that to our nearest and dearest, it may help us determine if we should spend our precious time making more money or giving more value to others.

When I think about the happiest, oldest, most generous people I know, they are not the wealthiest. It's not to say I don't have FOMO about spending a retirement cruising round the world or golfing and spa days, but I also know myself. I would be bored of that after a year. Staying active mentally as well as physically is the best way to retain health and vitality.

One of the people I most admire is an author called Barbara Hannay. Coincidently we live in the same town as I am writing this book. Barbara got her first publishing contract aged 47 after more than 4 years of trying and has written over 60 books. In her 70s she still produces a book a year under contract to Penguin. I find that amazing and I'm so grateful to have her example to follow. It proves that even in the middle stage of life our dreams can still be manifested through effort and using our natural talents.

Midlife can also see us wanting things to be as they were before and having to come to terms with the fact that we are not able to do the things we used to do for a whole variety of reasons.

Midlife also means perimenopause and menopause for women and OMG is that not a whole new world of self-discovery. Thankfully there is now scientific research to prove that women's brains, as well as their ovaries, change during perimenopause so if you start to think differently – it's because your brain IS changing!

The Blessings and Curse of Midlife

Dr Lisa Mosconi is the associate professor of neurology and radiology at Weill Cornell Medicine and is the first person to do ground-breaking research on the changes in women's brains during menopause. You may like to check out her book; *The Menopause Brain: The New Science Empowering Women to Navigate Midlife with Knowledge and Confidence.*

I certainly have noticed changes in my brain and body in my late 40's and I'm applying different tactics and strategies to help me manage the changes occurring in my body. Armed with knowledge and self-compassion you can hopefully come through menopause with energy and vitality. I certainly see a lot of examples of strong, active women on the other side of menopause. Personally, I chose to cut right back on alcohol and increase my intake of foods that contain natural Phytoestrogens.

Research shows estrogen may support bone health, mood regulation, and lower cancer risk in both genders. Let me point you to a helpful online article you can read to understand why we need to increase phytoestrogens as we age and what foods contain them naturally.

https://www.webmd.com/diet/foods-high-in-estrogen

Typically, I use western medicine as alternative medicine and alternative medicine (such as food and meditation) as primary medicine. The choice is yours and I'm grateful to know I have so many choices available to me.

Recognising Midlife

My husband is the same age as me. I won't talk about him too much else he may want some royalties from this book, but in trying to understand my own midlife changes I'm learning to be understanding of his. I don't try to change his mind about anything, but I do try to be a healthy example and hope that by seeing me taking care of myself, he feels curious and empowered to take care of himself too.

Several of my friends have lost their husbands to suicide, and I realised that the best we can do for each other as midlife adults is to enable and support each other to be healthy so that our loved ones don't have to grow old without us.

Many of us will have seen some classic cliche signs of a man's midlife crisis play out. And more women are starting to articulate their experiences of a midlife crisis using research, writing and talking about it. Hiding it, trying to be brave, going it alone, or just sinking into despair is not the way for either men or women to understand and accept that this phase of life is as challenging as puberty, and we probably have even more hair to deal with.

Well, congratulations on reaching midlife! I hope you will find the following chapters thought provoking, entertaining, compassionate and healing. All around the world, there are people just like YOU! And YOU are special, unique and wonderful, so go ahead, embrace midlife, embrace the changes and be KIND to yourself and others.

The Blessings and Curse of Midlife

Let's get into the juicy parts of health, wealth and speaking honestly about death. After all, I don't want you to come back to me and say, *"Why didn't you tell me about this!"*.

"What good is our security system if the Wrinkle Fairy can get in without setting off the alarm?!"

Chapter 2
Midlife Moments from Around the World

The Blessings and Curse of Midlife

A few people have trusted me to share their "Midlife Moments" with you for the simple reasons that you may see yourself in their story and feel more compassion for yourself and others. In the journey of life, many of us encounter the same struggles, and "curses" as others, even those on another continent.

Let's meet Edd - 51-years-young from the U.K.

"I think everyone has a change in health as time moves on, it's natural. I've recently lost partial hearing in one of my ears, no reason for it but one day I woke up and that was it. It's all about adapting with the new situation and keeping moving forward. Am I healthy? Not entirely, I'm carrying a bit too much weight and I don't eat healthily enough in general. My problem, like a lot of other people, is I like food that is not good for me, but I've been saying that I should change things for 25 years or so, but I still haven't gotten around to it!

If I wish I'd done anything different it would have been getting on the property ladder in my 20s but I worked in an industry that didn't pay well enough to buy a house or to pay into a pension, which wasn't offered back then, so I pay an extortionate amount on rent, I won't get too much of a pension, and will likely work past retirement age as I won't be able to afford to stop.

I actually left my old job a couple of years ago because my work life balance was appalling and, although it paid well, my days could last 14-16 hours, including working on weekends. My new job pays less but I get more holiday, less hours, my weekends are my own and there's certainly less stress. With rising living costs, I miss the money, but I just have to remind myself of how my life was back then and that puts things into perspective.

I dream of not having to worry about what happens when I can no longer work. It's a weight that gets heavier each year and something I don't have an answer for. If I have one stress in life, that's it. That said, it can't dictate how I live my life. I'm blessed to have a partner, still have my parents and, in the main, I have reasonably good health. My life could always be better, but it could so easily be worse, and I have it much better than a lot of other people I know and those I see in the news around the world. I'll continue to take one day at a time and not spend time dwelling on what might have been. You can't change the past; you can only get on and live your life the best way you can."

Thanks Edd!

Let's meet Antoniya – 42-years-young from Bulgaria

"When I turned 38, things suddenly started to change. It was as if someone had flipped a switch on my life, and I found myself in a whole new reality. My skin decided it was time to explore new textures, my body seemed to have its own ideas about gravity, and my emotions - Let's just say they were auditioning for a soap opera!

This change was strange, weird, emotional, and dramatic. It felt like I was living in someone else's body, and not in a fun Freaky Friday kind of way. It took me nearly two years to figure out what was going on. During this period, I made quite a few frantic visits to my GP, had heart screenings (yes, plural), tried diets, medication, and even CBT therapies, I had frequent flyer miles at the doctor's office but always tried to keep away from medication.

Dealing with the unknown brought its own set of challenges. The stress and anxiety of not knowing what was happening to me was overwhelming. Every new symptom felt like a mystery to be solved, and the constant worry took a toll on my mental health. I was caught in a cycle of fear and uncertainty, which only exacerbated my physical symptoms. It was a vicious circle that left me feeling drained and helpless.

About a year into this symptom ordeal, I got diagnosed with IBS - I managed to unlock an evil beast that secretly lives inside everyone. I'd never heard of IBS before, and oh dear, the number of people around the world that suffer from this "hidden" (but not always) condition is pretty remarkable. Suddenly, I was part of a club I never asked to join, complete with its own set of dietary rules and unexpected bathroom emergencies. Not to mention the effect it had on my work commutes every day, it was so scary!

Then, one day, my doctor looked at me with that concerned, professional expression and said, "You're depressed."

"What? Me? Depressed? Surely not," I thought. I absolutely disregarded the offer to start taking antidepressants. My stubbornness kicked in, and I was determined to take things into my own hands.

I embarked on a journey of self-care and exploration. I started meditating, exercising, reading, spending hours taking hot baths, and swimming - in other words, looking after myself. I even joined the gym - something I've always wondered how people can stick to. But when it comes to facing THIS kind of change, well, you need to try everything. And trust me, no one is prepared for it. Amidst the chaos, I found moments of peace and strength I didn't know I had.

Midlife is a weird and wonderful stage. It's like puberty, but with more wrinkles and less patience. It sneaks up on you and DEMANDS that you pay attention. And while my journey involved some hilarious missteps and awkward realisations, it also led to a deeper understanding of myself."

Thanks Antoniya!

Antoniya shares her experience of Dealing with Death in Chapter 6.

Let's meet Andrea – 47-years-young from Brazil.

"I watched my father and then my husband both become OLD due to work at an astonishing 38-years-old. So, it was an agreement between my husband and I that we would work hard for 15 years, and then try to have a child. This allowed us to progress a lot in our careers and travel the world (70 countries!). We decided to be disciplined about our finances, to save money and make humble choices while investing

(like a simpler car and home). We have waited and it paid off for a more comfortable midlife.

In terms of future goals and my legacy, this was a deep reflection that I had when I decided on a career transition, already with my baby daughter... what is my purpose, how can I make a difference in this world so that she has a better environment, and most importantly, as she grows and flies, when I look back what will make me proud? Where do I want to dedicate my time and energy? And I found this answer exactly in the conscious choices I made, with the help of an amazing career and life coach and dear friend, just possible by the financial structure that I built throughout my life. I now have a flexible career of advising strategy and governance for companies and leaders.

I will list my 5 important lessons, because their bond is, in fact, my secret to happiness...

1. GOD - *I really felt His support, I experienced some miracles and blessings in my life that make me very grateful, so have your spiritual faith to support you in this difficult journey.*

2. FINANCIAL PLANNING *for independence including passive income and asset diversification. My father was very strict and from a humble family, so I wanted to be able to have a better life.*

3. SIMPLICITY - *I am a very simple person, I have been through significant situations, such as almost losing my parents when I was 12-years-old, and almost dying with my daughter during my high-risk* *pregnancy, so maybe I have a different mindset and I adjust my energy and focus accordingly..*

4. ROOTS - *I have climbed very high in my career, travelled a lot, so returning to the family farm and enjoying that routine and the powerful simple life lessons from my relatives, like taking care of the health of my body and mind. This has kept me grounded, even in the midst of all huge challenges.*

5. GO AFTER YOUR DREAMS - *life is hard, so I have always tried to enjoy the journey and fight for my dreams NOW... not a future thing."*

Thanks Andrea!

Let's meet Anthony, 47-years-young from Hong Kong.

Anthony became a widower at 44. The father of two children he shares his experiences of coping with loss during lockdown in Sydney in 2021. You can read more about it in Chapter 6 – Dealing with Death.

"The last 6 months of 2024 have been very different from the last 3 years, with the biggest change for me, feeling ready and comfortable to invest in growing and learning with someone new. There is a new sense of excitement and energy, incorporating the lessons learnt from my previous marriage, with a view to a partner for life and knowing what I want with much more clarity than when I was in my 20s. I'm blessed

to have found someone that I feel so comfortable to walk the path of life, with trust and determination.

The kids also opened up on their views of a prospective pairing, both filled with joy, hope and some anxiety, which is to be expected. Their acceptance of someone new for me will vary in pace for the kids respectively, but they both understand and see my happiness increased during this time."

Thank you, Anthony!

Let's meet Cathy – 64-years-young from Canada.

"It really hit me when I moved, aged 46, to another country. When you are working and living in a continuum, although colleagues and friends come and go, there is still a core group of people who have known you since you were young. In my case since I left home at just 18. Those people see you as they have always seen you. They have aged too, but there is a tacit agreement that 'we are still the young people we have always been,' just maybe a bit heavier or a bit greyer. I left my old life at the top of my 'game' and full of confidence. In a new place what people see is you, as you really look: the people who gravitate to you are the same age, some older, but they all see a middle-aged person. You make the same judgement about them, not just in appearance but interests and careers and families. It forces the recognition of exactly where you have reached on the road - this is the Middle of the Dark Wood that Dante lays out, and it is a scary place.

As I went through my 50s, I found that I was trying to be the best at what I used to do, and that work had moved on whilst I was looking the other way. Technology, work patterns, assumptions of 'how we do things' change and if you take even a short break or change direction the change races on relentlessly: I was not the best anymore, not even close and that is a tough thing to acknowledge.

I have always believed, still do for the most part, that if you want more money then work harder. I have been blessed with robust health, a reasonable earning capacity and little interest in material goods. As my partner, who was 9 years my senior, became unwell, I became the sole earner, but I have always been the one who was good with money, so I just worked harder. State pensions kicked in for him and we trundled along okay, even though I had left the big earning international gigs behind for the most part. With no children it is easier to see the whole financial picture.

Shifting to more local, small-scale work here in my new home, which was a conscious and deliberate choice, meant that, when my partner needed more and more care, I was doing flexible work in a very supportive community. It felt stifling sometimes as I am used to a big build up, tear down and move on type of world. The more I needed to be at home for my partner the more grateful I was for my humble gig, and the less I had to spend money on travel, entertainment and 'stuff'. When you are trying to keep someone alive that stuff really must fall away."

Thanks Cathy!

Cathy shares her experience of Dealing with Death in Chapter 6.

Let's meet Louise, 57-years-young from Australia.

"I've been working hard my entire life and I'm now entering a new frontier. After surviving three toxic, abusive, long-term relationships I am again in a rebuilding phase.

I've experienced enormous financial stress and hardship due to my choice of partner's and each time I've had to work very hard to get myself out of it. I know that I am a survivor and will continue to grow and evolve however it has been extremely difficult at times. At 57 these experiences have put me off wanting a partner, although at times I feel extremely lonely. However, this time I'm determined to stay single and continue to work hard to ensure I have a secure future.

The rising cost of real estate, and homelessness statistics for middle-aged women are both frightening. I'm mindful of both as I try to organise my way out of a financial tangle with my ex-partner. Working in aged-care I see what life is like for many retirees and those that have little or no family support. I'm hopeful that I can find a new home and lifestyle that suits me and allows me to do all the things I enjoy while having a passive income in the future that will give me some further security as I age."

Thanks Louise!

I guess I should share a few bits of my midlife tale too and you will find more of my experiences throughout the book.

Hi, I'm Krissy 49-years-young from Australia.

"Having babies in my 40s messed with my earning potential for the best part of a decade. Realising I had compromised away my income and gained many health issues due to an unhealthy workaholic lifestyle in my 30s has been challenging. I used to refer to myself as a fat, middle-aged executive who travelled extensively, earnt decent money, and my waistline expanded alongside my income. I remember being in a nice hotel room in Spain (Seville), about to go for a few drinks with colleagues on the roof terrace by the pool, and I saw my naked body in front of a full- length mirror and I remember thinking: "Where did that come from!"

My lifestyle and other factors caused fertility issues for my husband and I, and I spent a small fortune to have my babies. I was very ill during my first pregnancy and the baby needed 1-1 care for the first few years of her life. This cost me another fortune in childcare as I hired a nanny so I could go back to work. In hindsight I'm not sure this was wise, but I didn't feel as though I had options, or the right supports to do it any other way. Living in another country far away from family often means you must hire people to help you do the things you may often ask family to help with.

I guess you could say I spent my children's future dowry on keeping them alive and, although I would not change that, it does force you to make decisions others do not have to make.

Ever since I was a kid, I was finding ways to make money doing chores and working the same jobs as adults. At 17 I had three paying jobs in retail, hospitality and real estate. That theme continued at university where I worked three jobs. I still have multiple jobs, side-hustles and non-paying work commitments and often my two children will ask me: "Mum, how many jobs do you have?" That question makes me smile, as we all know being a Mum is the biggest and hardest job there is.

It's no secret that our reproductive years are also our productive years, and I see so many women end up with very little in the later stages of life due to the sacrifices they made giving up their earning potential to raise their family, and then the husband leaves them with nothing. I've always tried to maintain some independence when it comes to money. I never want to have to ask permission to buy something or do something I want to do. I always pay my share of everything, but I also do think about how I will manage if things were to change in the future.

As I approached my 49th birthday I realised I have another decade of good earning years ahead of me, and I will try to maximise those. I had very little money in my 20s, pretty good money in 30s, OK money in my 40s, and I'm planning to be more financially astute and abundant in my 50s.

When it comes to my biggest midlife lesson it is **Health is Wealth**! I can invest time in myself which also pays dividends. I've created an active and passive income stream through my books and my investment property and hopefully I will continue to develop more money-making opportunities in the future. I've still got stuff to learn *but I trust myself to be OK and I'm going to work really hard to have a great relationship with my two children so they will take care of me when I'm older. That is my strategy at least. It does worry me that young people who go to university have so much debt and the prices of homes are too high for most young people. My legacy to my children is that I will try to leave them one if not two properties that they can live in thereby having a home to build their own path.*

When I exercise, I see two kinds of older people. Those being pushed, and those walking, jogging or swimming, and having coffee with their friends. I do know which one I want to be, and it is this reason that keeps me getting up before my family each day. I studied Exercise Science and Sports Management at University. I represented Australia at three world championships in my 20s, and worked on three Olympic Games, and two Soccer World Cups. I know a lot about sport. What I did not learn at university or anytime thereafter were the tools for wholistic health (mental, physical, spiritual, emotional, financial). In the past five years I've become an avid student of wholistic health and wellbeing, and this has been the biggest gift I could have given myself. I want to talk about, write about, and share what I've learned to help others, both younger and older.

My books and blogs speak to people because they are relatable, readable and helpful for unpacking common problems. I don't mind talking about the hard stuff. I want to generate good conversations around common issues. My pet hate is when people use the word "moderation" because I firmly believe this concept is only causing our health crisis to worsen and our society relies on Sick Care as opposed to Health Care.

As I've become more open and vulnerable in sharing my stories, others share with me and I'm grateful to have people who value my work and trust me with their stories."

Likely, you have your own Midlife Tale to tell, and it could be related to any of the points shared by our friends above. Health, Wealth, Work and Dealing with Death! These common themes are explored in more detail in the following chapters. Every time I feel overwhelmed by the craziness of life, I remind myself of all the FREE help, support and services available to us, and I relax because I do know that there are good people all around us who can offer help, if we ask.

The loneliness epidemic is real and those that are lonely live shorter lives than those who are not. Do consider your social environment and connections at different stages of your life. As someone who has lived and worked all over the world I sometimes wonder if I would have more friends if I had not have travelled as much. But I decided on balance that I've been lucky to meet amazing people all over the world AND the world is transient. Therefore, I will continue to meet more amazing people as I enter new phases of my life and hopefully, I will continue to travel.

Midlife Moments from Around the World

"I have to work late again, but don't worry —
I outsourced our love life to a couple in India."

My notes and reflections

Chapter 3
Health in Midlife

The Blessings and Curse of Midlife

Have you heard the expression, *"If you don't make time for Wellness, you have to make time for Illness?"*.

I'm quite certain that if you are mid-aged then you will have a few creaks and groans, and your health may be starting to suffer from one of the many things we have been exposed to over the past few decades. For instance:

- Chronic stress.
- Convenience meals.
- Sitting down for +8 hours per day.
- Lack of quality sleep.
- Joint, bone or muscle deterioration.
- Toxic environments (people and places).
- Caring responsibilities 24/7 x 365.
- Limited high-impact or strengthening exercises.
- Difficult relationships.
- Addictions - food, alcohol, shopping, gambling, gaming.
- Decreased collagen, estrogen and testosterone.

You may have received a letter from your doctor when you turned 40-something asking you to come for a check-up. In this chapter we are going to consider wholistic health in midlife and hopefully your take-aways, (ideas, not food) will be that you start to seriously consider your health as your number one goal in the decades to come.

Health in Midlife

Dr Greger is the best-selling author of, *How Not to Die* and *How Not to Age*. His friendly and informative advice on nutrition, sleep, fasting and disease is empowering for anyone wanting to understand their own health and well-being. You can find his work at NutritionFacts.org

I like to think of my body as my House, and I am constantly paying the interest living in it. What that means to me is that I want to live in this "House" comfortably as long as possible, and the healthy interest I pay to my body will pay me back. Every decision I do, or do not, make in respect of my body has a compounding effect. We know that compound interest builds quickly, silently and it can become an unsustainable investment or loan. Just like our middle-aged body. Life has crept up on us and all those decisions we made (or didn't make) in the years before become very obvious as our health may be in decline.

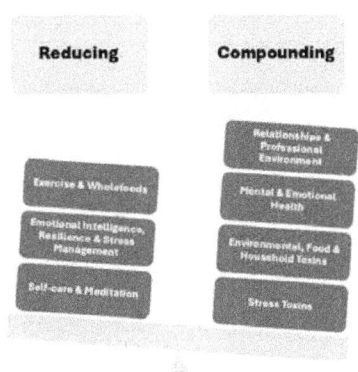

Compounding Interest

I too was a person who didn't pay attention to my health in my 30s and after a decade my body started to fail me, because I failed it. I failed to take notice, I ignored signs in the mirror, and I mindlessly lived in a body (house) that I paid no attention to while I hustled at work, socialising, and enjoying uninterrupted TV marathons. I continually exposed my body to all of the compounding things listed above and I very rarely practiced wholistic self-care.

Let's talk about Self-Care for a moment. Do you even know what that is?

I had never heard of self-care until aged 45, now it's all I see. The challenge is that many of us don't know how to relate this concept to our own individualised circumstances or life. Self-care is about Self! You are yourself! Do you get it? You can't carbon copy someone else's self-care plan and think you will become miraculously healthy.

I created a **Self-care Needs Analysis,** and this gave me all the answers I needed to refocus on my health and wellbeing. I also started to think more about my Sustainers and Drainers and how I could lean into activities that sustained me to even out the unavoidable things that drained me. I became a student of mindfulness, and I discovered the more effort I put into being mindful the healthier I became, physically as well as mentally. A regular Self-care Needs Analysis, or Life Audit, is helpful to remember your priorities and realign your care plan. The simple questions with *Yes/No/Sometimes* answers can provide all the information you need to get yourself back on track with your self-care.

Action	Yes/No/ Sometimes
I aim for at least 7 hours sleep each night.	
I have good boundaries in my personal and professional life.	
I understand my Sustainers and Drainers and can adapt my self-care plan to meet my own needs.	
I embrace a Wellness Mindset.	
I am able to switch off thinking about work or doing work and be fully present with family and friends.	
I make time to exercise 3 times per week.	
I nourish my body with healthy food.	
I manage my consumption of alcohol.	
I am not dependent on pain medication.	
I recognise my need for personal development and connection, and I don't feel guilty about investing in myself.	
I balance my own needs with my family's.	
When I feel overwhelmed, I take a break and look at the situation with objectivity.	
I detach from my emotions, and I don't allow my feelings to take over.	
I get impatient easily and have a short fuse.	
I feel that I'm doing it all on my own and I don't have anyone to help me.	
I know how and when to get support if I need it.	
When life feels busy and out of control, I use my breath to anchor me in the present moment and know that "This too shall pass."	
thewellnesspoet.com	

After consistently balancing my self-care plan my life has changed completely.

- ✓ In my late 40's instead of tv marathons, I run marathons.
- ✓ Instead of socialising in bars, I offer retreats.
- ✓ Instead of worrying, I choose to wonder.
- ✓ I buy antioxidant rich foods, instead of thinking about how to get rich.

- ✓ I limit my exposure to toxins and keep good boundaries.
- ✓ I practise a Wellness Mindset, so I don't have to spend time dealing with Illness.

By aged 42 my health was not good. It was pretty bad to be honest, and I thought there was a very good chance that I would not be around to see my girls grow up, and that I would become just another sad statistic. That revelation changed my attitude to many things in my life and thank God I had time to undo all the damage I had done to myself.

I take full responsibility for my own poor health as I am the person living in my body. Of course, not every illness is our own fault, however, if we pay good attention to our body and take care of it, then there is a very high likelihood we will avoid many common illnesses and diseases. If we think, eat and believe the same things as our parents then it makes sense that we have the same genetics as our parents, however science now tells us that we do have a lot of control over our genes, and we can influence them through our thoughts, feelings and nutrition. To do this we may need to let go of many misconceptions about food, emotions, exercise, what we can and can't do, what is actually relaxing and what is not, and how much effort we should put into living our best life now versus saving up for retirement.

There are a few times in my life when I have checked out of "normal" life to focus on my health and well-being. At the time, I made a conscious decision to invest some time, effort, and money into taking care of myself. This investment paid off many times over and I will do it again in the future should I need to. In my early 40s I realised I needed to build a new foundation for health and create a mindset for wellness regardless of how busy I was. I replaced the idea that I was too busy with work, kids, life, family etc. with the idea that I could live longer and healthier and have more time for everything and everyone if I took care of myself.

The first time I checked out of normal life to focus on my health was aged 41.

I had a young child, had just completed a horrendously stressful project with people who did not care about me, and instead of going on a well-earned vacation to Greece I got Chickenpox. That illness nearly killed me. After I recovered from Chickenpox we went on our delayed vacation to Corfu, and I got Norovirus. I spent my 41st birthday with my head in the toilet.

On the second last day of the holiday, I was brave enough to put my little child into Kid's Club and my husband and I had an hour to ourselves.

Our sun loungers were positioned not more than 60 meters from the Kid's Club so I could sneak back and peak at my daughter. I remember telling my husband with 30 minutes to go to, *"Hurry up and relax!"* We only had half an hour to relax as hard as we could! After I got home from that holiday I was peeved off! I was still exhausted, still sick, and still not sleeping from that traumatising job. After a traumatic pregnancy and very difficult first 2 years as a new mum I was spent. Life felt pretty crap!

I was between projects and indecisive about what to do next. I was just too burnt out to feel passionate about going back to work. I applied for jobs, went for interviews and got rejection after rejection. I wondered what I was doing wrong. Then one afternoon I was sitting at traffic lights in Tooting Broadway, London and I suddenly had my epiphany!

"You need to take a few months off! You need to go to yoga, swim, rest, be mum, and do sod all till you feel well again."

I decided right then and there the date that I would go back to work, with no idea what work I would go back to, but I would not look for work for the next 2 months. And guess what? I got well, I got fitter, I was reenergised, and I was offered a job without even applying a few weeks later, and I started just after the date I had set myself to go back to work. That job lasted six years and provided me with lots of amazing friendships and connections and the opportunity to train staff at Buckingham Palace. The chances are I may have never been ready for that opportunity if I had not taken a break.

The second time I checked out was a year after child number two came along. I was 43 at the time and had not long moved my family home to Australia (phase 1 of midlife crisis). My health was very poor again, as neither of my children ever slept well and I had chronic insomnia. I had continued working hard, not sleeping, not exercising and not eating well. I was overweight, I had breast cysts, adrenal burnout, and non-alcoholic fatty liver disease (mostly non-alcoholic).

I could have surrendered and thought, I'm too fat, too old, too sick, too tired, I wet my pants when I sneeze, I don't eat this, and I only eat that, and I'm going to suffer all the aged-related lifestyle health conditions as many others. BUT another epiphany arrived one day when I was dressing my daughter for school and I suddenly realised that if I did not get healthy, I would not be around to see her finish school.

- ✓ I started running, it hurt.
- ✓ I cleansed my gut.
- ✓ I studied mindfulness and practised meditation.
- ✓ I cut right back on meat and alcohol and increased my intake of plants, nuts and seeds.
- ✓ I prioritised rest and sleeping when I could.
- ✓ I cut back my hours at work.
- ✓ I started journaling and unpacking my emotions.

After 8 months of prioritising my health, I had zero health conditions. I was fit, healthy and happy. I wrote my first book, ***Broken to Unbreakable, 12 Steps to an Unbreakable Mind, Body & Spirit.*** This book charts the 12 steps over 12 months that I created to reclaim my health and wellbeing. I continue with these

The Blessings and Curse of Midlife

12 steps in my life today and have had 5 amazing years of good health without any visits to the doctor.

The third time I checked out to prioritise my health was aged 48 ¾. Which is right now, as I write this book. I've experienced so much in my life that it was time, once again, to share it with others. After a few very busy years of working and raising small kids, I acknowledged that my wellbeing was suffering as perimenopause was kicking in. I always take full responsibility for my health as I know what it feels like to be super fit and super fat. I'm not judging anyone for either but feeling super fit is incredible. It's just very hard to sustain while working and raising a young family unless you are on the Olympic team (which is basically your job anyway). I could no longer run away from the onset of menopause with my bodily aches, mental frustrations and emotional health keeping me awake at night.

Now, unless you are super rich, taking some time out to focus on your health is going to cost you something, and I know that not everyone can do this. But let's imagine for a moment that you don't prioritise your health and you become sick; you may even develop a life-threatening illness from not taking care of yourself. In my mind, this is a freakin' tragedy. It's tragic that we get sick and die from doing life because we didn't have any time-out to take care of our health.

So, how do I justify the cost (investment) in taking time out? Well, it helps that I have some experience in this topic as I've done it a few times already. But the biggest thing you should think about is trusting yourself. Trusting that this time and investment you are making will pay off. Any costs associated with giving yourself time to be healthy will pay you back. It has for me and I'm certain it will for you as well.

I know that we were not put on this planet to rush around, working every day, not spending time with our family, becoming overweight, burnt out, and sick so that the world could prosper! I don't subscribe to that channel any longer.

In the same way it's impossible to maintain fitness if we don't exercise, or maintain our weight if we rely on takeaway, it's very easy to lose our health. Throughout my 40's I've noticed a cycle of improved health, followed by poor health, and when I think of the conditions surrounding both I am very aware of the circumstances that led me to be either healthy or unhealthy. I'm not just referring to physical health either because difficult circumstances can bring on challenging thoughts and emotions which cause us to suffer.

It's widely recognised that emotional health is the key factor in many major illnesses. Constantly cycling through difficult emotions and unhelpful thoughts is keeping us stuck in an ongoing cycle of poor health. If your life is busy 24/7 and you have a lot of responsibilities, processing your thoughts and emotions is probably not something you have considered doing. It's important to understand the emotional wheel and the hormones that are associated with those feelings. Being mindful of our feelings, and the hormones they generate is critical to understand our physiological response to stress and its impact on our body.

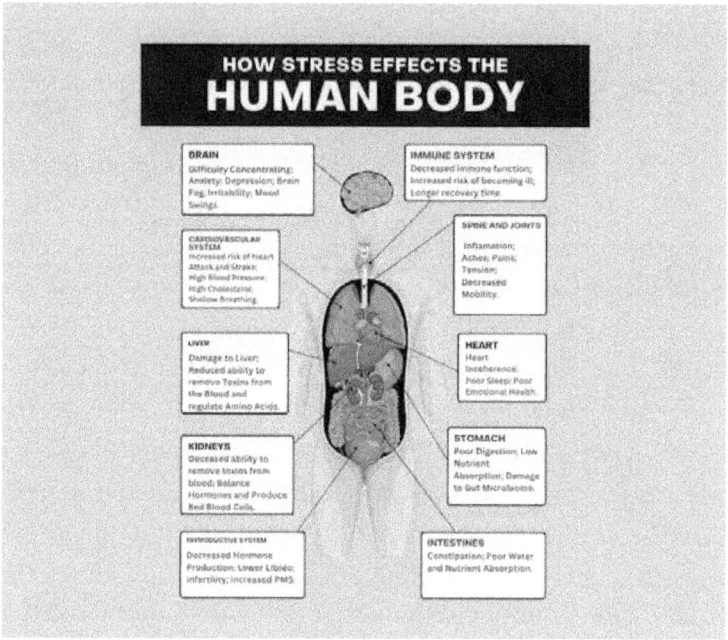

This simple graphic on how stress affects the body was a game-changer for me as every time I feel stress creeping into my life this image comes to mind, and I quickly try to de-stress myself.

When we understand the compounding effects of stresses on our body (physical, emotional, environmental) and how it affects our internal organs, we have a very easy decision to make regarding our desire to be stressed.

Throughout the day you can check where you are on the Emotional Wheel, taking care to spend more time in the Mild and Pleasant quadrants as these quadrants keep our body in balance. You can and will notice your emotions in the other quadrants and it's important to acknowledge these emotions, process them, reflect on your state of mind and your relationships, and then choose how to move forward in a helpful way, causing minimal harm and suffering to your body.

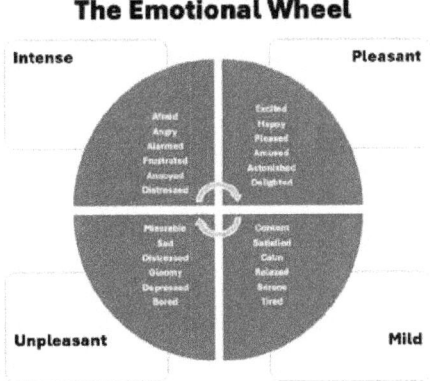

Wouldn't it be amazing if we all learnt tools to process and manage difficult emotions in order to prevent major life illnesses? I am an advocate for talking about emotions, taking time to process emotions and healing. Doing so is difficult but far less work than managing a serious illness such as cancer or autoimmune disease.

Learning about Wholistic Health is one of the best gifts you can give yourself and your family. Of course, you can still buy them cake and mini muffins, but you will find ways sneak health into their day too.

My girls and I love yoga before bedtime, and they don't know I'm thinking about how many different nutrients I can squeeze into their meals each week. We talk about our emotions; we cook together and walk to school as much as we can. They see me running and I encourage them to enjoy their activities while making time for my own. I don't compromise away all my free time to rush them from one thing to another.

I recognise my need for "alone time" is an important part of my self-care routine and I forgive myself for all the mistakes I make when I am a tired, shitty parent. I practise self-care every day, dipping into the different buckets of self-care; physical, emotional, spiritual, social etc.

I embrace a Wellness Mindset to enable wellbeing as my primary goal, even when I'm busy. I honour my body and try to train my mind to help me achieve my goal of good health. I could very easily think myself out of good health by not being mindful of the thoughts I'm having which dictate my behaviours and choices. On Sunday, I ask myself the 10 questions in the graphic below aimed at preparing myself to be healthy for the week ahead. I call it Proactive Wellness or a Wellness Mindset.

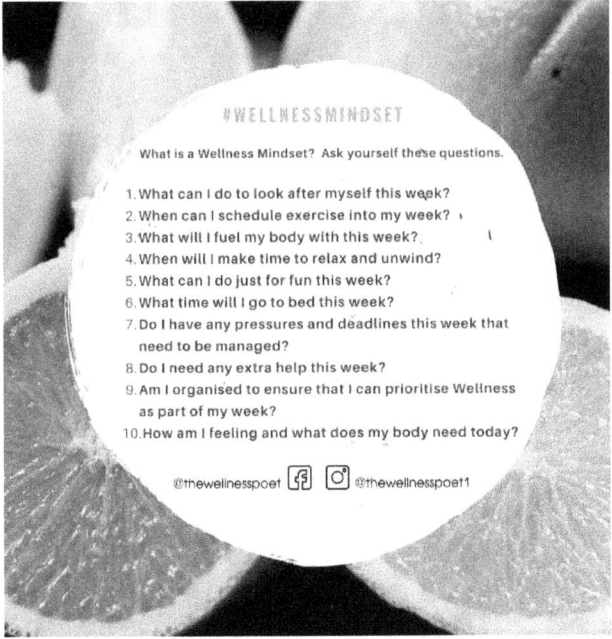

I engage in FREE Health and Wellness. I consume free content on the internet, and I create my own. I walk, swim or jog in nature. I practice meditation at home, and I cook most of our food.

All this FREE stuff saves me time, and money, and I have more time and money to invest in other things I love to do. Travelling, spoiling my children, creating books and cooking amazing food. I also support other Free and Low-cost Wellness Warriors who are using their experience to help others. Good Health should not be expensive or only available to those with high incomes.

My top 10 tips for Health in Midlife are;

1. Ask your Wellness Mindset questions every week.
2. Prioritise Sleep.
3. Understand your Habits and Behaviours.
4. Understand your Stress responses.
5. Create some firm Boundaries in work and family life.
6. Put your Health and Wellbeing first.
7. Ask for Help.
8. Exercise, Stretch and Meditate daily.
9. Eat food that Nourishes your body.
10. Laugh, Learn and Share.

The best way to be healthy in midlife is to be responsible for yourself in mind, body and spirit. We know that mental health is a problem faced by many. We know that obesity and, consequently heart disease are problems faced by many. But what about Spiritual Health?

The definition of Spirit is: *the "non-physical characteristics" of a person.*

What are your non-physical characteristics?

- Kindness
- Compassion
- Authenticity
- Joyfulness
- Having a Purpose
- Being Open-minded
- Having a sense of Humour
- Being Social
- Being Appreciative
- Belief in a Higher Power

Too often we forget about Spiritual Health in the non-religious context because we are focused on financial health, mental health or physical health. But the non-physical parts of us are a gateway to all the other part of us, so please don't forget about them.

My midlife friends receive funny videos and memes from me throughout the day because I want to bring humour into their life, let them know I'm thinking of them, and hopefully bring a smile to their face. When we smile, we remind our nervous system that we are safe, and our breathing slows down and we feel calmer.

It is said that 6-year-olds laugh 160 times per day. At 49 I AM the mother of a 6-year-old, and I too want to laugh 160 times per day, not the average of only 6 times for an adult. As I edge ever closer to 50, I'm finding more things to laugh about, I'm running, swimming, eating and resting my way to good health and I hope and pray that more middle-aged people will do the same.

Toxic environments, toxic people, and the toxins of stress are killers. Understanding toxins could save your life and help you heal your body. I've been on a journey to understand toxic people and to heal from narcissistic abuse. 15-20% of people have narcissistic personality disorder so sadly you are likely to have met some. In contrast 1 in 4 people suffer sexual abuse so imagine the compounding effects of both narcissism and sexual abuse in your life.

Dr Ramani is a leading expert and author on narcissism and provides lots of helpful tips and insights in how to recognise them, how they impact us and how to heal from them. It's very powerful and important information because narcissists can show up in our work life, home life and in our own family.

According to Dr Ramani narcissism is the second-hand smoke of mental health. She details 6 types of narcissists and the traits they exhibit. As I've said before, knowledge is power and it's free on the internet, so do educate yourself about how narcissistic colleagues and family members maybe impacting your life, and your health. You can view Dr Ramani's work here: https://doctor-ramani.com/

There are times in life when we may be hustling, studying, raising a family, single parenting, dealing with grief, or just feeling zonked and we don't have capacity to care for ourselves. I get it! I know

Health in Midlife

that my family love me, however they are not experienced enough to help me be healthy, so I need to do it for myself. I need to be my own spokesperson, and advocate for myself. We should never compare ourselves to others because we really don't know their circumstances at home, but we can design a health plan which is adaptable to any situation. I've seen many people become healthy and strong despite all obstacles, and you only have to look at our Paralympians to know that anything is possible if you put your mind to it.

I partnered with Randy Glasbergen to give you a midlife giggle as I find his comics about life really funny. You can check out his full catalogue at: https://www.glasbergen.com/

"After all these years, I'm finally comfortable in my own skin. Maybe it's because my skin is a lot bigger than it used to be!"

My notes and reflections

Chapter 4
Wealth in Midlife

The Blessings and Curse of Midlife

Money is never far from the front of your mind in midlife.

- Do you have enough to retire?
- Can you afford to pay for your kids' tertiary education or wedding?
- Is your house paid off?
- How many credit cards do you have?
- How many grandchildren do you have?

In midlife money matters come into focus and many of us were never taught the art of investing, or desired to become entrepreneurs with tax advisors. Jaspreet Singh talks about those that climb the corporate ladder vs those that own the corporate ladder. In medical school he realised he did not want to become a doctor because none of the richest men in the world had gone to Uni to get a degree to have a job. At 19 he bought his first investment property, and now he teaches others how to invest with his 6 Steps to Wealth Formula. You can check out his work @minoritymindset.

In this chapter we will talk about Financial IQ and Financial EQ, and you can consider your relationship with money. It is also useful to consider the times in which we now live and all the factors in your life that have impacted your capacity to earn; as well as your mindset relating to money.

You may have heard of Ken Honda the famous Japanese writer who wrote ***Happy Money*** after he made enough money to retire by the age of 29. Ken's advice and wisdom on money are invaluable especially with anyone grappling with the idea of how much money is enough and how many "followers" you need in order to make a liveable income. Ken has popularised the idea of Thanking Money for its contribution to your life. Thanking the inflow and outgoings of our money as if it's doing us a favour by being in our lives. In appreciating money, and what you have, you attract those people and opportunities that also appreciate money, and then the flow of money, both in and out, becomes a harmonious process instead of something to worry about.

A money coach may be able to help you understand your relationship with money or resolve any limiting beliefs so that you can overcome blockages: attracting and keeping hold of your money.

My personal attitude is simple. Money comes, and money goes! Sometimes really rich people lose all their money, and sometimes when you have been really poor, a few years can go by, and then you are really well off.

I confess that I'm not hung up on money. I don't obsess about it, nor am I ultra cautious with it. When I have it, I spend it. When I don't have it, I live with what I have. I have had a relaxed approach to money as throughout my life whenever I needed money, I got a job, worked hard, made some money and carried on with my life. I've slept in my car when I had no place to stay, I've sofa surfed with friends, and I once I even slept on a dog's bed outside my friend's house after my grandmother, who enjoyed her pain medication with a few bottles of XXXX, picked a fight with me. In contrast, I've also lived in 5-star hotels, and apartments with harbour views. I do have a tent which gives me the reassurance that I will never be homeless.

I was not born into a wealthy family and, so far, have not inherited a chunk of money. My parents are generous with what they have and have worked very hard. I couldn't save much when I was younger despite working and earning since the age of 13, I do not have a huge pension waiting for me. BUT I'm not worried about any of that because, whilst I haven't come from money, and my financial IQ may not be as high as some, my financial EQ is strong and generally I can make good decisions when I must. Financial emotional intelligence (EQ) enables individuals to recognise and acknowledge their emotions related to financial stress. It encourages self-awareness and intuition when it comes to money matters.

I also know my value, and my worth, so I don't measure myself against what others have. I do what is right for me and my family. I believe in investing in yourself and being financially independent from your partner and family. Of course, you can accept help and support if you need it but being financially dependent on someone (including your employer) generally opens you up to some form of abuse. Financial abuse is one of the most common forms of domestic abuse and women are often the ones who suffer the most if they have taken time off to care for children and family members. Financial abuse keeps women stuck in a cycle of poverty.

Nomadland is a 2020 American drama film written, produced, edited and directed by Chloé Zhao. I expect thanks to Covid it's not very well known, but do watch it if you can. It's about a woman in her sixties who loses her husband and then her money, and finds herself in a van as a Nomad, travelling around America. She makes friends with other Nomads who all seem to know where to find the seasonal work. What I enjoyed most about this film is that these Nomads value what they have, they are not dwelling in misery, and they tend to appreciate other people for who they are, not what they have.

The idea of being a nomad or a gypsy sits OK with me and having lived in seven countries and travelled to more than forty I've seen firsthand the happiness of people living with very little. I do like good food; nice bed sheets and I no longer buy the cheap wine. I'm at an age where I know that life is too short to drink crap wine, and since I drink very little wine these days it must be nice, or don't have it.

In midlife we have an opportunity to ask ourselves some good questions when it comes to money.

- Do I hustle hard for money, or do I let it flow?
- Do I take advantage of people or situations for money, or do I act with integrity?

- Do I overspend and try to impress people with money or materialistic things?
- Am I conservative or tight with my money?
- Do like seeing lots of money in my bank account?
- Am I too generous with my money?
- Would I lie, cheat or steal for money?
- Do I weaponize money against my partner, family or employees?
- Do I worry about having enough money until I take my last breath?
- Do I fight with my family over money?
- Do I get jealous of people who have more money than I do?
- When I see someone smashing their financial goals am I happy for them?

It might take you a while to answer these questions honestly, but I do think it's healthy to audit your feelings and relationship with money, and to build your financial EQ muscle to cope better with financial stresses. There is a lot of very helpful information relating to financial EQ, freely available on the internet, do check it out.

Financial stress and debt generally are the cause for most relationship breakdowns and as we mindlessly go through life not learning the tools to build financial independence it can feel very overwhelming. Sickness, marriage breakup, children with health problems or other life factors often cause money stress too. Like with health, I would encourage you to be compassionate to yourself (and honest) about where you are on your money journey and find support where you can.

Often money is used in families to create "conditions" for love. Families fall apart over money all the time, mostly in adulthood when a relative is nearing the end of their life and money is involved. This whole situation makes me immensely sad and uncomfortable. Gifts of money are wonderful but not at the cost of relationships.

Some people have amnesia when it comes to money which is also sad. We see that money controls politics, healthcare, the media, and companies are generally trying to come up with more ways to get us to spend more money on things we shouldn't need. Natural resources are exploited for money, people are exploited for money, and money corrupts just about everyone. To a degree I would say that money uses us, we don't use money. Which is why I like to think that Ken Honda's advice is healthy.

Ken Honda reminds us of the pitfalls of continually trying to chase more money, investing more, taking bigger risks and so forth. He says that the people with higher Financial IQ are more at risk of losing their money because they can be obsessed with making more money. In contrast those with high Financial EQ are less likely to lose all their money as they can spot scams and will not take unnecessary risks.

The Blessings and Curse of Midlife

It's relatively straightforward to learn some skills to improve our Financial IQ and indeed there are many books written about how to invest our money, retire early, and all that jazz. I know people who've written books about financial independence. However, what I also see is that financial independence doesn't necessarily mean you don't experience loneliness in your old age. Being frugal in your 40s doesn't make you a more fun person in your 60s. What I've witnessed, and read about, is that as we age, we begin to make poorer decisions around our health, and wealth, and start spending money on stuff we don't need.

Why did I end up sleeping on a dog's bed at the age of 17 when I had gone to live with my grandmother? Because I was getting in the way of her having a good time with her boyfriend who in his 70s and 80s was spending money on fast cars and impressing his friends at the Club, and she thought he was a great bloke. 30 years later my granny died in a nursing home alone during Covid. I was the one that cleared out her room, organised her funeral and wrote her farewell poem (eulogy). How people treat us is more valuable and memorable than anything they can ever buy us.

At times I've been way too generous with money; when I should have been saving, I was giving money away. When I should have been investing; I was spending to impress.

On the flip side, I've always had capacity to earn money when I needed it. I've manifested money and opportunities that many people dream about. I've taken risks and trusted my instincts and have often found myself the receiver of very generous gifts and opportunities. I trust in the ebb and flow of money. Sometimes you have it, sometimes you don't but if you need it, it will find you.

In the west we are very lucky to have active charities and a lot of government funding, including access to free healthcare, welfare and so forth. I take comfort in the fact that there are literally so many avenues to find help, support, money, and food that we should never live in a mindset of scarcity when it comes to money.

I have a good friend who has been financially abused into homelessness on more than one occasion and left in a lot of debt. She worked hard, dug herself out of it and is now sitting on several income generating assets. If she liquidated her assets, she would have more than $1.5mil in her bank account. A lot can change in a short space of time, and it is this knowledge that also gives me comfort when it comes to the ebb and flow of money. Our wealth is very much linked to other decisions in our lives.

When I bought my first house in the UK (aged 29), my husband and I had been married less than a year and we were not earning much money. We were lucky to get a 100% mortgage. I instructed a totally useless firm of solicitors who almost messed up the purchase of our small ugly house, but thankfully someone with a heart and a brain got involved and managed to get the documents completed on time. She also informed me that since the house was valued under a certain amount, we did not have to pay stamp duty, so we saved some money on that too. On transfer day the bank messed up and sent the money to the wrong account and so the sale almost fell through again. It was all so incredibly stressful, and I couldn't understand why it all had to be so hard.

After we bought our house, we were even more broke, and the property needed so much work to bring it up to a decent living standard. The first room I wanted to renovate was the hideous bathroom. I worked for seven weeks without a day off and saved enough money to kickstart the bathroom project. Over the course of the next few years, room by room it took shape. During this time, we had decided to move to a bigger city (London) to save money on the cost of commuting. Based on our income at the time we needed a massive deposit to get a second mortgage. So, I lived off my credit card for one year and saved all my income as the deposit for the second house. We moved again into an ugly house that needed a lot of work and set about room by room renovating it (and I paid off my credit card). We now had a new home, and an investment property.

A few more years went by, and at this stage I was pretty skilled at understanding the property market, and the behaviour of estate agents. I told the agent I wanted to smash the ceiling price in our neighbourhood for the sale of our first house. And we did! We used that money as a deposit for our third house which has since been sold and we are now mortgage free on our fourth house while our second house provides some monthly income.

I never had a big dream to be a real estate investor, however each of those opportunities and decisions came from acting quickly with instinct, and this is financial EQ. I value my financial EQ more than any tips or hints from financial gurus who may or may not wear shoes! I have worked with many global financial institutions, so you could say that I should be more invested in Money, but I was also in the boardroom of major Banks in London during the Global Financial Crisis (GFC), so I tend to trust myself first and foremost.

Most energy gurus will tell us that money is just energy, and we can tap into the universal flow of money by raising our vibration and surrounding ourselves with likeminded people. Of course, I understand this, I also understand that abundance is not just about wealth. Abundance is about appreciating all the gifts of life. Our attitude to money is generally indicative of our attitude to most things in our life. It's IMPOSSIBLE to be happy unless we can respect and appreciate simple things in life and often money can make things so darn complicated. We can be generous with our time as much as we can with our money, and time is money.

You may have also heard the expression, "our Network is our Net worth". Yes, it can be true, but a superficial, disingenuous network won't genuinely care if you are there or not.

I choose to be generous with money, and time, because I've experienced so much generosity in my own life, and I value those people and experiences more than I can ever express in words.

The Blessings and Curse of Midlife

When it comes time for someone to pack up my final possessions, I would like them to remember that while I was alive, I gave them everything I could so that when I was dead there was very little work for them to do. Packing up my 93-year-old granny's things in the nursing home after she died was a very sobering activity. I just remember thinking 93-years of life fits into a few garbage bags when you are gone.

My children ask me where we will live when they finish school. I picture myself a bit of nomad, travelling the world in a small van, with a bicycle, stopping off to see all the amazing people I've met who've added to the rich tapestry of my life. My husband may or may not choose to do this with me, we don't drive well together.... But as long as I have a tent, and a good heart, I know I will be OK.

With retirement age increasing, and the cost of living rising, many of us Gen X are less well off than our parents. According to experts our children will be even less well off. Working into our 80s might be the norm. Hence, **Health and Wealth** are inextricably linked.

I am an admirer of Jack Canfield who wrote Chicken Soup for the Soul and is a world-renowned motivational speaker and founder of the Transformational Leadership Council. In 2024 Jack is 80, he is still working, has a fantastic podcast, and is still helping people all over the world. From humble beginnings as a high school teacher who visualised and manifested his way to millionaire guru. Side note – he has been married three times and his eldest son wrote a book about his horrible life growing up the son of Jack. You can't be perfect at everything, I guess!

I meet many people still practising their side-hustle in their 70's and I admire them. Hobbies which generate income, provide access to community, friendships and travel can help with health, wealth, and longevity. If you can turn your hobby into a means to sustain you in some way throughout the rest of your life, I would strongly recommend you do so.

A comfortable retirement is a dream for many and we can "kill ourselves and lose our selves" while trying to earn that. As you will have read in Chapter 2 some of our friends have had good and bad experiences when it comes to finances. You should never judge yourself or others when it comes to money. Like I said rich people can become poor in the blink of an eye and the vice versa. It is said that generous people get more done!

My final tips for Wealth in the Midlife are.

1. Increase your financial IQ to understand how you can invest and grow your wealth.
2. Build your financial EQ so you can better adapt to financial stress and make decisions more aligned with your values.
3. Invest in yourself to earn and learn as you age.
4. Invest in your Health as well as your Wealth.

The Blessings and Curse of Midlife

5. Don't judge, appreciate what you have, and learn to tap into the universal frequency of money.

"On your last day of work, you get to keep all the returnable cans and bottles in the break room. That's our pension plan."

Chapter 5
Work in Midlife

The Blessings and Curse of Midlife

We are in a new phase of professional development with the rise of AI and systems that make many humans redundant. When I was a child, someone was paid to fill up your petrol tank; now we can pay at the pump. We scan our own groceries, book our flights and publish our own books. Life is a little more equal for men and women; but faster, busier, more accessible and stressful than ever before.

Working in our midlife may differ slightly for men and women however one thing I notice often, is that it's a time of change for both sexes. We begin to question our professional choices based on money, time, fulfillment, family, health, lifestyle etc.

Our 20s are generally a time for learning how to work, in our 30s we work to rise, and in our 40s we may reach the heights we have aspired to, or we begin to plateau. Our time is divided between raising our family and potentially taking on caring responsibilities of older relatives. The juggle between professional fulfillment and family obligations is constant and usually the person that suffers the most is you, by either not meeting expectations, or your own potential.

On the flip side it's possible you've risen high enough at work to call the shots, run your own business and choose who you work with.

What we want to do with our life is a question that keeps coming up in our 40s.

- What do I want to be after I've grown up?
- Do I have the new skills needed to keep pace with this changing world?
- Do I have the energy to work like I did in my 20s and 30s?
- What can I do to make more money, and have more time with people I love?
- Am I doing work that brings meaning and fulfillment to my life or am I grafting for a pay cheque.
- Do I need to gain more qualifications, or do I need to see a career coach?
- Is my current workload/job/profession sustainable as I age?

I'm fortunate to have worked with some amazing men and women all over the world. I've had some incredible work experiences and some absolutely crap ones too. The people I aspire to emulate in the future are those that are doing what I want to be doing, in their 60s and 70s. Clearly, they went through their midlife professional transformation and either reinvented themselves or crafted a life that enabled them to make a living from their passions.

Leadership skills in life as well as work are important for self-actualisation.

Work life challenges are different for each generational cohort and where you were born. Sadly, in the 2020's there are many global conflicts and more refugees in the world than ever before, somehow talking about fulfillment at work could be seen as a luxury.

Dr Alexis Abramson, an expert in what are known as 'generational cohorts', says that when you are born affects your attitudes, your perceptions, your values and your behaviours."

I am a proud Generation X, born between 1966 and 1980. I grew up in a time when technology was advancing fast, but it wasn't nearly as readily available as it is today. Because of this, I straddle both the digital and non-digital world and understand the importance of both. Accordingly, I am resourceful, logical and a good problem-solver.

I also have a few other things on my side. I grew up on a farm, was home-schooled until aged 11 and started earning money doing chores aged 7. On the farm I cooked from scratch aided by recipe books, cleaned the house, helped grow vegetables, milked cows, butchered animals for food and entertained myself for many hours, week after week, month after month, year after year. By the age of 17, I was holding down three jobs and I had three different income streams throughout university.

It might surprise you that I gained OK marks at school, obtained a science degree, travelled the world working with many blue-chip companies and was even paid to train staff at Buckingham Palace. I don't know of anyone else that shares my same story. My resume is long, diverse, and I call myself a jill-of-all-trades, master of none.

Work in Midlife

And I am 1000% happy with my skill set. I don't want to change it; the challenge is trying to find work that uses it all, and values it all.

I was quite successful professionally in my 20s and 30s and backed myself when I needed to. I quit jobs when people were toxic and was brave enough to go to foreign countries on my own just for the experience. I have lived and worked in seven countries doing a variety of life-enhancing jobs, and whilst based in the United Kingdom for sixteen years, I had the chance to work and visit more than 40 other countries. There is something very vulnerable and humbling about being alone in a foreign country, especially in the days before mobile phones. You were truly present in your own life and had to rely on purpose-made human interactions to survive.

This is not a travel book, although I do have many travel adventures to write about in the future. I will however relate some work experiences that have been life-changing in the hope that you too feel OK about questioning your choices when it comes to work-life balance.

In 2003, I travelled to Poland from Sydney for the World Dragon Boat Championships. This was the third and final time I would represent Australia at a world championship. I had been working in Sydney for an international food company. I quit my job and headed to Poland, saying goodbye to my then boyfriend (now husband of 20-years). The plan was to compete at the world

The Blessings and Curse of Midlife

championships, travel around Europe for a while, meet up with my boyfriend to see if we still liked each other, and maybe stay away from Australia for 2-years. I had a backpack and a bag with two paddles when I left Sydney. I returned 16-years later with two children and a shipping container! So, what happened in those 16-years aged 27 to 42?

Back in 2003, I quickly ran out of money after the world championships, drinking too much beer in Prague and coffee in Venice. In a hotel in Rome, I found a job online as an English Teacher in Poland. I messaged my boyfriend to say I was coming to London to get a visa to go back to Poland and teach English. We met up, got engaged, I got my visa and embarked on a very weird journey back to Poland with no phone, acting on trust alone. Two Polish men (strangers) met me at the airport in Frankfurt to drive me to the school. Several hours into this journey I started to wonder what the hell I was doing. I was dropped off in a tiny town in the middle of the night in Poland. You would never allow your own daughter to do this!! My parents had no idea.

After a few days alone in a typical post-war apartment, my roommate arrived, another Aussie, the same age as me. Thankfully we got along great. We taught English to NATO soldiers, factory workers and children. We travelled all over Poland experiencing the incredible scenery and the generosity of strangers. At that time Poland was also in a transition from post-war soviet influence to joining the European Union and I fell in love with it. I made a promise to one of my students to help her in the future if she wanted to leave Poland and work abroad. A few years later I delivered on that promise, and decades later she lives in New Zealand with her husband and daughter.

Those four months teaching English (Australian) to Polish people in that tiny town gave me an insight into how things might have been before and during the second world war. I saw poverty and resilience everywhere. I felt so grateful to have grown up in a safe place where I had choices of where to live, work and play. I also saw the optimism of young people hoping to have freedom and choices to learn English, join the EU and to fulfil their potential. I saw large families living in small apartments and making do with what they had.

It is a privilege to cross two time zones and to witness the before and after during periods of rapid change. Ten years later I worked in Ukraine and saw the onset of their change which then abruptly ended by a new war with Russia in 2022. I have so much sadness for the lives of my Ukrainian friends whose careers and lives were ended by this total madness.

In 2009/10 I went to work in South Africa for the Soccer World Cup. I had many moments of being alone in a car in areas with no other white people. Literally the only white woman in the village. I never felt afraid. Maybe it was instinctive, but I only ever experienced loving help and laughter from those I met and the joy of getting to know them, and their lives, made me see the world very differently. I saw that faith, hard work, discipline, and respect are the values of many different races of people and in contrast to what I was led to believe growing up: we are all the same. I love that.

Adventures during my travels have helped me make sense of many things in my life. Of course, I've made many mistakes, but I like to think of myself as a conscious global citizen who can feel empathy for other cultures and gratitude for the smallest act of generosity which, when you are alone, goes so far.

By midlife your choices around work probably start to align more with your personal values and professional integrity. Sadly, there are those that lack both and you will probably have met and worked with several by the time you arrive at your 40s and 50s. Regardless of the industry or profession you have chosen you have likely experienced workplace bullying and toxic behaviours.

Dr Joe Dispenza researches and talks openly about the health epidemic caused by mental and emotional health conditions. And, since we spend the vast majority of our lives at work, or commuting to work, then we can assume that many health conditions can be attributed to our work environment. It's no joke that at work you are just a number, and, should you not be able to make it, there is always someone that can take your place. People will feel sad for your loss but you will just be another statistic.

Work in Midlife

The best way to make sense of challenges at work is to remember that WORK is not all of you. Work is just one part of you. Ruminating on work or allowing toxic behaviour at work to overpower your life, and impact how you show up for your family, is just NOT worth it.

Many of us have dealt with workplace liars and bullies. Emotional, psychological and verbal abuse at work is common and sometimes physical abuse and even rape. In 2022 the Workplace Health and Safety Act was updated in Australia to include psychological safety. Of course, it won't eradicate all instances of workplace abuse, but it might just help educate victims on what actions they can take when they have negative experiences at work. This is a positive change which I'm grateful for in my lifetime, added with a new law that allows employees to switch off and not be available 24/7. If you struggle to keep good boundaries in your work, it will quickly permeate all aspects of your time. Covid and remote working escalated that, and the impact will be measurable in the years to come.

Many of us derive our personal value from our achievements at work, forgetting that our hobbies, homelife, and relationships are also important achievements. Based on my experience the latter three (hobbies, home and relationships), become more valuable in midlife as we start to wonder how we can spend more time doing the things we love, with the people we love.

The Blessings and Curse of Midlife

Many great friendships are formed at work; however, these friendships can be a moment in time, something that you did together, overcame, or endured together and those friendships may only last a season. Once life moves on those friendships may too. In contrast if you have the same job for decades, it's possible you've grown up with your colleagues and there is a lot of safety in sticking with people who know you. Work can be an amazing place to express yourself, challenge yourself and grow as a person.

From a women's perspective a lot of things change when you become a mother. Your desire to be away from home changes, your need to nurture your children instead of your clients shifts, and you may also want to work in a way that enables you to be there for those special moments in your child's life.

Of course, not every woman has the luxury of choosing to sacrifice money over special moments particularly single mothers with limited support. When my daughter was in year one, I took some time off "regular work" to write this book, and to just be "Mum" after a particularly busy year. I did this with the support of my husband and in full knowledge that my income would be negligible for a few months, but I needed this time to write and regain my vitality, and I wanted no guilt whatsoever.

One day the school held a special celebration, and parents were invited to pay a bit of money to experience a cultural activity. I wanted to share in this special day with my children, so I paid the money, we dressed up and went along. Afterwards I was settling my young child into her class and the little boy sitting next to her complimented her on her outfit. He then said that he couldn't afford to have the celebration breakfast. My heart split into a thousand pieces and I felt guilt of another kind for the entire day. I would have happily shared our breakfast with them had I have had the chance.

I share this story because I think it's important to acknowledge that all around us people are living through different circumstances and experiences, and at any moment we can be them, and they can be us. Choices in other areas of life may dictate the choices we have in work or, depending on our role-models growing up, how we view our capacity to make money.

My granny also grew up on a farm. However, unlike me, her mother would not allow her to finish high school, represent her region in sport, or follow her dreams. She worked in a milk bar, was introduced to my grandfather, a war veteran, married and had two kids and then spent her 30s, 40s and 50s cleaning motels. She was a homeowner at the age of 25 and savvy with money. As a child all my clothes came from the Op shops (second-hand), or she made them on the sewing machine. She grew all her vegetables in the garden and had an active social life. She was a great tennis player and very good at knitting and crochet. In contrast her cousin, a man named Lew Hoad, followed his passions and won the Wimbledon Tennis Championships twice in singles and three times in doubles. He is less famous than Ken Rosewall but arguably his life is more interesting. Sadly, he died of cancer aged 59 in Spain where he had a tennis ranch visited by all the movie stars of time.

My granny died aged 93, she did not climb to dizzying heights of achievement or fame, although I did write her biography in 1992 as my year 12 English project (I got an A), and I now have a copy of Lew Hoad's biography. I wonder what would have happened to my grandmother if she had a different set of parents. If you think about the ending for those two cousins, who won in the end?

I gave birth to my first child aged 39 after I had achieved all the goals I'd ever set in my professional life. I worked on three Olympic Games, two Soccer World Cups and met many of the famous people I'd admired growing up. I travelled extensively, earned good money and had many enriching life experiences thanks to my work-life. Sidenote, it cost me a lot of money to make my babies, but it was worth it.

And here is what I've since learned: There is no free "pre and post parenthood career transition service" for women? Hmmm!

Anyway, the life of a jet-set mummy is not so sustainable after the birth of a child with special health needs. And so, I had to let go of that. I tried to keep doing the same job but sleep deprivation, and the intensity of the workload was too much with a small child at home. Remote working was largely unavailable at that time. I found myself trying to lead a project which was fraught with disaster due to its naïve design and poor leadership. I tried to quit a few times but loyalty to the client and my ability to do hard things meant that I kept going when I should have stopped. That experience changed my mindset about work forever. And aged 41 (at the time) I realised that I was not going to put myself in danger personally or professionally ever again. Nowadays, when I see red flags in the workplace, I check my exits and back out accordingly. It's just not worth it: my children need me.

Having arrived in my 40s with a baby I determined that I needed a SAFE mum job, and I went back to University to get a Diploma just for a piece of paper as proof of what I had already been doing for years, so that I could apply for other jobs. That all worked out OK for a few years until baby number two was born. I was just too exhausted and rundown to hold it all together. I had to officially acknowledge that in midlife all the stress, working, sitting, eating, drinking, IVF and not sleeping in my 30s and 40s had caught up with me and I was very ill. Midlife health alert!

It was then I decided not to prioritise work and income, but to focus on the importance of joy and hobbies instead. This has culminated in six published books, an income generating side-hustle, and lots of new friendships all over the world. I know that AI can write books, and assignments, and poetry and songs. However, what we know about storytelling is that it should help us feel something. People are NOT marketing funnels.

The Blessings and Curse of Midlife

Not all of us are lucky to achieve our career goals: perhaps due to illness, injury or other limiting factors in life. However, if you are lucky enough to have arrived in midlife with a reasonable education, access to opportunities, and a few good social assets on your side, then you may face those typical midlife work/career questions that I faced.

John Robbins was the sole heir to the entire Baskin Robins fortune and empire, but he gave it all up, becoming an environmentalist and living off-grid. He went on to write a best-selling book about How Your Food Choices Affect Your Health, Happiness, and the Future of Life on Earth.

His book, ***Diet for a New America,*** was one of the first books to explain why a typical American diet that was dependent on meat, dairy and factory farming was unhealthy. The book became an international bestseller. Robbins was wealthy again. Years later when his father was dying of heart disease his then Doctor unknowingly recommended a copy of his own son's book. Thereby reigniting a relationship that had been strained for decades. John had made his own path and impact on the world.

This story always gives me inspiration to follow my own calling and not to work against my values. Most self-help gurus and personal development coaches will encourage you to visualise your future achievements in order to manifest them. There is a famous story of Jim Carrey writing himself a cheque for $10mil for Acting

Services Rendered and forward dating it 10 years. 10 years later he was paid $10mil for his movie Dumb and Dumber.

I believe that many of us have the privilege to reinvent ourselves throughout our life and still achieve anything we set our heart to. I take courage from stories of men and women in their 80s who take up new hobbies and make money doing things they love. I feel that life is punctuated with opportunities, pauses, achievements, downtime, creative time, active time, hustling time, regenerating time, and we can embrace each of these moments mindfully, learn from them and emerge into the next phase of our life.

Midlife gives us an amazing opportunity to audit our work life with knowledge, experience, and hopefully some agency about how we want to spend some of the best years of our lives. I'm OK with a grace period for rest, reflection and reinvention. I like storytelling and helping people, and I hope these two things will sustain me well into my 80s. I visualise a "go anywhere I choose" life that allows me to write, coach, speak and share what I have learned all over the world.

I'm grateful for all the horrible bosses, meaningless jobs, and diversions I've had in my work life as they have led me to appreciate my time and my efforts so much more when things go well. Believe me: there is nothing more empowering than picking up your handbag and walking out of a toxic workplace knowing you don't ever have to go back. If you are a good person, you will get a new job, or your family and friends will help you and, when all else feels lost, I remind myself that there are soup kitchens and that brings me comfort.

During the 2008 Global Financial Crisis when my industry was crumbling, I was asked to go to the office of someone who had not treated me particularly well in the months prior and sit at a desk pretending to work so that their client would not see that they were struggling or had no staff. I turned down that generous offer, noting to myself that I would rather go to a soup kitchen than play an office mannequin.

There is a high likelihood we have had to stay in a job too long because we could not afford to leave, or we believed we needed to put up with being treated like dirt because we desperately wanted to gain experience from this person or that company. We have all had to be nice to horrible people at work whether that was our boss, colleagues, or clients. It is not always possible to quit when things do not go your way, but we generally know that working in a job you hate with people who make you feel sick, will actually make you sick… so, do yourself a favour and think about the following.

- Conduct an audit of your life skills and work skills and decide which ones you like best and which ones have served you well in the past.

- Think about someone you admire who is older than you, doing things you would like to do and then listen to what they have to say.
- Ask yourself, is appreciation or remuneration your driving force in life?
- Write down your personal values and then ask yourself if you can live those at work?
- Do you bring your whole self to work each day, or do you wear a mask and pretend to care about stuff you do not care about for a payslip?
- Have you missed precious family time to be with your clients or colleagues and if so, was the sacrifice worth it?

Ultimately, you should not squander your health and happiness for more money and greater sacrifices unless you are truly sure this is what you want.

There are many genius minds, great leaders and inspiring adventurers who have given us the life we have today. BUT in your life, you are the boss, and whatever you choose to do should be right for you, at any stage you choose; even if you decide that right now, you want to simplify your life and let go of all the trappings of too much credit, not enough time and too few precious memories. Just do it!

If on the other hand you are finding your second wind, finishing a new degree and ready to take on the world, go for it… with full knowledge and agency that you can wind up, and wind down, whenever you need to. Do not be afraid to start again and give new things a go.

I have several friends and former colleagues older than myself who I have observed trying to hold on to a career that they could no longer keep up with. It is sad to watch this and a useful reminder to myself that jobs and careers are not forever. There is a great movie with Robert De Niro and Anne Hathaway called, The Intern, a 2015 American comedy-drama film directed, written, and produced by Nancy Meyers. Essentially the older, experienced man (the Intern, who is trying to be relevant in a young person's world) prevents the young businesswoman from giving away her power and reminds her what she loved about her business in the first place and encourages her to trust her instincts.

As we age, we want to continue to be relevant and useful in a younger person's world. But we must also not devalue our experiences and contribution. Thinking about our legacy is a good idea: giving back to our community with our skills, knowledge and mentorship of younger people is truly valuable.

Over the past few years, I have been trying, sometimes successfully and sometimes not, to use my skills to help young people in my community. My message to young people is simple: it does not matter where you came from, you can go wherever you want to in life.

Work in Midlife

Whilst I usually give freely of my time, I have decided that in the future my valuable help is valuable, AND good role-models are important at home as well as work. In the coming decade I will focus my efforts on preparing my children for the future by exposing them to different people, experiences, opportunities, side-hustles, and I will encourage them to use their unique gifts and talents to bring joy to other people. I will also try hard to learn from them so that I can keep up with them in the future.

"I'm an expert in crisis management.
I've been married for 25 years and raised 3 kids!"

My notes and reflections

Chapter 6
Dealing with Death

The Blessings and Curse of Midlife

Dealing with Death is one of the downsides of midlife adulting and I don't want this chapter to be too sad, so I've asked some friends to help me bring some perspectives to the blessings and curse of midlife when it comes to death.

I will start with some of the blessings of dealing with death.

A death in your life can mark a period of extraordinary change. It can open up feelings of love and gratitude that were not in focus before. It can be a reminder to cherish special moments and memories, and to love with no remorse. A death can signal a new beginning or an opportunity to start over. It can give us strength and power to challenge systems and invoke change. We can learn and grow from our experiences dealing with death and we can be the one who listens quietly when someone needs us.

At the midpoint of my life, I am a friend to many widows and orphans. Clearly, I had not thought about this earlier in my life and the profound responsibility of this means I have become more selective about where I place my attention and to whom I give my time.

I know that grief manifests in many ways and that women, more so than men, are socially expected to carry their grief longer than men who can move on with less judgement. Any woman I know who has become a widow has been judged harshly for finding a new partner in the hope of moving on with her life. In contrast I've seen men celebrated for remarrying and moving on with life.

Dealing with Death

I have no idea why this phenomenon exists, but I would like to call it out. It sucks!

Where there is death there is usually a lot of stuff to sort out and this creates work, stress and often breakdowns in other relationships. Sometimes there is blame, anger and more suffering. When we are at our most vulnerable and in the most painful part of our lives, we may feel most lonely and isolated.

Grieving is such a personal thing there is no way to stereotype the grief from losing someone you love and, in the immediate aftermath of loss, you may not have the words to ask for support, or to ask to be left alone! Depending, on the circumstances of death the trauma may live with you for decades so not only are you suffering with sadness and grief you may be dealing with trauma, flashbacks and PTSD.

In all instances it's important to be compassionate to yourself and, as much as possible, those around you, who will be coping in their own way. Honour the stages of grief and don't try to go it alone if at all possible. Talking about your loved one to those who knew you both can be very healing, and a reminder of special times. Everyone who has lost a parent and must console the other parent through grief while navigating family dynamics and trying to maintain life for your own family, will understand that it's practically impossible to get anything right. Relationships can be forever altered by death leaving many with ongoing residual suffering.

The Blessings and Curse of Midlife

For every friend of mine who has lost their partner to suicide they attract far more anger and ongoing resentment from their partner's family than they ever deserve. It's heartbreaking to watch this unfold.

I think it's important to remind ourselves of some of the myths and facts about grief and grieving.

Myth: The suffering will go away faster if you ignore it.

Fact: Trying to ignore your pain, or suffering, and keep it from surfacing will only make it worse in the long run. For real healing, it is necessary to face your grief and actively deal with it.

Myth: We need to "be strong" in the face of loss.

Fact: Feeling sad, frightened, or lonely is a normal reaction to loss. Crying doesn't mean you are weak. You don't need to "protect" your family or friends by putting on a brave front: showing your true feelings can help them and you.

Myth: If you don't cry, it means you don't miss them.

Fact: Crying is a normal response to sadness, but it's not the only one. Those who don't cry may feel the pain just as deeply as others. They may simply have other ways of showing it.

Myth: Grieving should only take a year.

Fact: There is no specific time frame for grieving. How long it takes differs from person to person. Typically, anniversaries and special occasions are very triggering.

Myth: Moving on with your life means you have forgotten about the person.

Fact: Moving on means you've accepted your loss but that's not the same as forgetting. You can move on with your life and keep the memory of someone as an important part of you.

Being stuck in a long-term cycle of grief can impact your health, relationships and wellbeing. While no-one should "just get over it", it is important to acknowledge how grief may be affecting you. The last thing the one you lost would want is for you to suffer yourself into poor health.

Dismissing and diminishing grief based on the age of the person who left us is also not healthy. For instance, losing a relative who lived a long life can be just as painful as having a miscarriage. Losing your partner to suicide can be as traumatic as your partner losing a long battle with an illness. Losing your child in a tragic accident is life-stopping and earth shattering.

When it comes to death, it's no surprise that it will happen to all of us at some stage. I wonder, then, if it's realistic to think through some scenarios about how you may deal with death if it was to come your way unexpectedly. Most of the planning for death is usually tied to money stuff like insurance policies. And in the writing of this chapter, I started to receive some ads for Funeral Cover - *Protect Your Family from Unexpected Funeral Costs with Seniors Funeral Insurance.* Helpful, thanks Google!

What if we asked ourselves some pre-emptive emotional questions around grief.

- How would I cope if I lost my spouse/partner?
- Who would be my "Go To" person if I had overwhelming grief?
- Do I have capacity to care for elderly relatives and what things are in place should they die?
- If I lost my child tragically, how would I process this pain?
- Do I believe in the afterlife?
- Do I believe in reincarnation?
- Am I a good support person to others dealing with grief?
- Have I researched the "stages of grief" so I can recognise signs in myself and others?
- How would I support my children if they lost their other parent?
- What would be the impact if I lost multiple people in my life in a short space of time?

If you are unsure about the 5 stages of grief, it's a good idea to remind yourself what to expect.

- Denial: "This can't be happening to me."
- Anger: "Why is this happening? Who is to blame?"

- Bargaining: "Make this not happen, and in return I will ____."
- Depression: "I'm too sad to do anything."
- Acceptance: "I'm at peace with what happened."

I'm reminded by someone experiencing grief that not everyone will complete this list or follow this prescribed order. The same person told me that on a visit to the bank her financial advisor was too timid to be honest with her about her finances as her partner had died leaving her with a decent sum of money. On the way home she treated herself to a more expensive bottle of wine having seen the advisor's notes highlighting that she needed to spend more money!

Antoniya who we met earlier and who reminds me to do my taxes every year, lost three people very close to her in a short space of time in 2023 and 2024. She articulates the pain she endured during that time and what she now carries with her and wanted to share it with others.

"How does one navigate through such overwhelming grief? What kind of human heart heals through so much sadness and pain? The initial phase is a whirlwind of shock and disbelief, where the reality of the loss feels surreal and incomprehensible. This is often followed by an intense wave of sadness, a deep mourning that seems to touch the very core of your being. During this period, every moment can feel like an insurmountable challenge, and the weight of loss can be utterly paralysing.

Gradually, a shift begins - it has to, otherwise things can turn pretty bad for someone and everyone else around them. There comes a phase of realisation, an acceptance that death, as much as it pains us, is a part of the human experience. It is in this phase that gratitude emerges, and power - to live for them, to do for them, to act the way they would have acted. We start to cherish the memories, the lessons, and the love shared with those who have passed. Reflecting on how these individuals have shaped us, we recognise the indelible impact they've had on our lives and our growth.

My father's lessons on kindness, generosity, resilience and honesty; My friend's vibrant spirit and dedication to her family; and my husband's auntie's unwavering determination to set a positive example—all these qualities live on within me. They have become a part of my internal compass, guiding me through the darkest times and reminding me of the strength and beauty that life holds.

Grief also teaches us the resilience of the human spirit. The old adage, "What doesn't kill you makes you stronger," rings profoundly true. The process of mourning and healing equips us with a fortitude that we might never have discovered otherwise. It's a strength born out of necessity, one that helps us move forward, carry on, and even find joy and purpose once again.

In a world that is constantly throwing challenges our way, from personal losses to global crises, it's this inner strength that sustains us. It's the memories of our loved ones, the values they instilled in us, and the love they shared that fortify our spirits and inspire us to keep living fully.

As I continue my journey, I hold close the wisdom imparted by those I've lost. Their legacy lives on in my actions and decisions, in the kindness I extend to others, and in the resilience, I muster in the face of adversity. Through this, I honour their memory and ensure that their light continues to shine brightly in the world.

Grief, no one is ever fully prepared for it, but it is an inevitable part of life. So is the strength to overcome it. By embracing both, we find a way to navigate through the darkest times, emerging stronger and more compassionate on the other side." Antoniya Beyriyska.

Cathy who we also met in Chapter 2 shares the pain of losing her partner after a long-term illness, she is also the editor of this book. We met while working together in China on the Olympics in 2008 and she never forgets a birthday. One true work friend, and Aunty Cathy from Canada as she is known to my two girls.

"I lost my long-term partner in 2023, I was 63. I cared for him during his 5-year illness with Chronic Obstructive Pulmonary Disease (COPD). I cannot say that I didn't resent the role, quite often really, but his safety had to be the first consideration in any choice I made. I imagine being a parent is similar. When that role is taken away, brutally, horribly painfully, you no longer have a 'first consideration'. The things that I used to slip into my days, with his encouragement, to bring me pleasure: a coffee outside a cafe, a visit to a gallery, a walk by the shore, are now available all the time if I want them. And I

don't care. What I have learned is that over half of the enjoyment was in having something to bring back, like a treasure or a gift: news, things I had seen, the nicest pastries. I took the pleasure so as to share with someone who was house-bound for more than four years and that made it worthwhile. Now that it is 'just for me' there is less than half of that enjoyment left, and it hardly seems worth the effort. I write the 'shared things' in a book each day, like a one-sided conversation, but it is scant help.

Being bereaved has left me living alone with a woman I hardly recognise: the last time I was on my own I was 22 - that girl is gone, I'm not sure I would even know her if we met - and the person who is left is half of a whole that has grown and rounded over 41 years into a world. If you cut that sphere in half the half that is left can't stand up, it lolls on its back like an upturned tortoise - the cut side exposed and browning in the air.

People, kind, decent well-meaning people, friends and colleagues and neighbours try to 'cheer you up' and I know that they absolutely want to help but, especially as time passes, that help becomes really intrusive and, sometimes, resentful: they have done their best, they want you to share their understanding of happiness and 'normal'. I can't pretend, though I try, to care about the things they so kindly offer (so much food) but I am being dishonest. They have to go on with that understanding of 'cheerful' and 'happy' because it is the foundation of their world, just like mine once had a foundation, but it is not, at least for me, a transferable commodity.

Dealing with Death

So, for me, I know I am blessed: I am dealing with my loss in a peaceful, beautiful place with good healthcare and relative prosperity. I am not going through this in a raggy tent in Gaza or the shell of an apartment block in Kharkiv, I know this, and I am grateful (though the gratitude can easily add to the guilt). I know I have had, and continue to have, an immensely privileged life but no amount of 'raindrops on roses and whiskers on kittens' philosophy makes a blind bit of difference to the emptiness of reforming yourself at the end of your life. I know it is, by definition, the fate of half of every couple in the world but, I would say, if you are trying to help someone 'through it' please don't assume that what you think they need is what they want or even what they can bear." Cathy Joyce.

In February 2021 a good friend passed away leaving her husband Anthony, (also my friend) and two young children. Both were friends from my paddling days representing Australia and we had spent many long days and nights together, cold, wet, and pushing our bodies to new limits. It was a huge shock when she left us. I was not able to attend her funeral, but I did say goodbye to her in my own way. Since Karen's passing, I've watched my friend, Anthony (her husband) grieve, raise their two children, be a single parent in Sydney during lockdown, and overcome the worst possible time of his life. He was open to sharing his story with us and I'm grateful that he entrusted me with his feelings and words, and I know his wife (my lovely friend) would be proud of him.

The Blessings and Curse of Midlife

July 2021

"*In the early days, I knew it was adrenaline that kept me focused on completing what must be done. I might seem strong and brave, but I don't feel like that at all.*

Sometimes I have the strength, feeling brave to carry on, albeit for a bit of time, then I stop and breakdown. I inevitably recover and eventually start up again. This cycle is happening more frequently now, this is my reality.

Tidying up has been one of the hardest things and really drives home the reality of it all. The kids are so resilient and strong, I draw on their strength to keep a routine, no matter how exhausted I am, but sometimes I am too spent. I've tried to help the kids and myself, refresh little things and keep other things to commentate that time. I think we've all benefited from that a bit.

I'm also looking for signs around to probably give me comfort that Karen is now doing OK. I really wish and hope this is true. I must believe that. Maybe she is trying to communicate to me, maybe not, but my senses are heightened at the moment.

I remind myself of the words I'd share with Karen during the difficult stages in life and now remind myself… 'In life, we have got to live looking forward, not backwards, we might occasionally look back to ensure we learn, repeat the good stuff and avoid the bad stuff, but we can't move forward just looking back. Consistency and balance are important, like watering a plant, it needs the right amount of sun, water and fertilizer, too much of anything will kill it, it's the law of nature.'

These lessons are very hard to apply at the moment."

October 2021.

"The first wedding anniversary passed by and I looked to keep a low profile about it, though my energy levels were low and higher stress. It was great to be able to catch up with a couple of guys leading up to the anniversary and on the day.

Coincidentally it was also the first time I've dreamt about seeing Karen directly in probably 6 months. Being aware in my dream that she is gone, it was confronting and filled with mixed emotions. She was smiling happily and gave me a cheeky wink from afar, which seemed to balance sad repeating thoughts I had in the weeks prior.

Single parenting has been a massive challenge, both looking to get their own attention and typically without much break for me at times. I know I need to also change my own paradigm in providing balanced advice and support for a budding tween boy and teen girl (with all the good and bad attitudes that come with that). By and large both kids have been resilient and supportive as they progress, and typically look out for each other as priority when we're out and about.

I'm trying my best to reset this year in preparation for a big 2022 as my focus to support the kids' schooling and continued growth will be *my main focus and driver. I'm glad there are times I have hope in my mind, they balance out my sorrow and grief."*

November 2022

"Just a few reminders for myself this coming year."

- Never forget your purpose.
- Be humble, determined and gracious.
- Set the right routines to be sustainable for life.
- Completing things the right way is more important than just results.
- Reflect on the legacy you want for all interactions.
- Actions speak louder than words, but aligned words and actions are the most powerful.
- Nurture everything around you in a positive and sustainable fashion.

October 2023.

"24 years between drinks to graduate again. When I started this journey, the purpose was, 'Why not?'. Between jobs and boredom, it was just something to do. During the journey life as we knew it changed, and I had many reasons to quit my MBA with new priorities. After work, getting the kids fed, and sorting their various activities, my energy and focus was at zero..

However, I found a different purpose with this. It was not about learning anything new, not about any self-achievement. That didn't matter to me. My new 'Why', was purely demonstrating to my kids that no matter whatever setback life throws your way, you never give up. Finish what you start and do it to the best of your abilities. Empower yourself to choose your own response in action, regardless of good or bad things that happen. This is the most powerful lesson I hope to impart on my kids."

January 2024

"2023 was a steady year at work and home. At times, I felt I was simply going through routine, not regularly motivated, mixed with positives and negatives. Energy levels were a rollercoaster ride, which were felt at home and work alike, resulting in what seemed to me an inconsequential year.

This year's social circle for kids was in a state of flux, with the normal challenges of teen experiences. They were both brave when faced with choices that aren't straightforward, as we talked through the pros and cons of their potential decisions, with the key principle of spending time with people who provide a positive and nurturing environment with balance. I also became more insular in some aspects, but also wanted to open myself up for a new experience. I know I will need the kids' support as I look toward my next chapter in this regard. I have not felt this energy and excitement in a long time, which I hope is mutual.

We ended the year with our first major overseas holiday to England without Karen. I shared some of the experiences that I know she would have wanted the kids to try.

As 2024 begins, I'm confident that I'm ready to move on with my personal life, with an eye for the future. This exciting spark will motivate me to get focused again for enhancing the nurturing platform at home, focused outcomes at work, and time for myself, as I look to incorporate a balanced and healthier lifestyle, both mentally and physically. I know this will be a positive influence and experience."

July 2024

"The last 6 months have been very different from the last 3 years, with the biggest change for me and feeling ready and comfortable to invest in growing and learning with someone new. There is a new sense of excitement and energy, incorporating the lessons learnt from my previous marriage, with a view to a partner for life and knowing what I want with much more clarity than when I was in my 20s. I'm blessed to have found someone that I feel so comfortable to walk the path of life, with trust and determination.

The kids also opened up on their views of a prospective pairing, both filled with joy, hope and some anxiety, which is to be expected. Their acceptance of someone new for me will vary in pace for the kids respectively, but they both understand and see my happiness increased during this time.

Dealing with Death

I do think that finding a partner during this stage, besides for my happiness and not growing old alone, will also benefit our respective kids, as we can set a good example of what a happy family could / should look like, as a major part of their childhood and influential years have lacked this experience.

For this, I'm grateful and hopeful of the future years ahead." Anthony Mak.

What Anthony's story tells us is that a midlife tragedy is both crippling and transformative, and he has been tested in every way possible. His commitment to routine, personal reflection and growth is both remarkable and inspirational.

My story of dealing with death in midlife relates to the miscarriage of one of my twins.

"I was blessed with a twin pregnancy after my first go at IVF. The excitement of seeing the double heartbeat during a 6-week scan was everything I had been dreaming about. I bought a book on twins, and feverishly started planning. The pain of all the needles and trauma of poking and prodding was forgotten replaced with joy and anticipation. A letter was sent to my local hospital informing them of a twin pregnancy and I was contacted for a consultation with the twin's midwife.

At 10 weeks I told my family I was pregnant with twins eagerly looking forward to my 12-week scan so I could see the babies again. The day of the 12-week scan was one of the worst days of my life. As I lay on the table the sonographer was scanning to measure two babies. At first, she was happy and chatty, and my husband was standing beside me. She did some broad sweeps of my stomach, and I immediately felt her energy change. She was silent.

She then asked me, "Has anything happened?"

"No." I said choking back tears.

I could see one waving, wiggly baby (Twin A) on the screen above me and one shrivelled peanut. The tears started in floods, and she quickly did her measurements and left the room to find a counsellor. I don't remember the context of that conversation, nor what happened afterwards. Shock, I guess! I stayed home from work the following day and cried in my bed. Then the guilt started.

I should be grateful I have one baby; I should be happy for that one baby. I needed to see that little baby again so I can celebrate in its life and try to move forward with a positive frame of mind. I booked another private scan and spent a Friday night with my baby.

As the weeks progressed, I tried to feel grateful that I still had one baby. But it was very painful. The twins midwife insisted that she look after me and thank God she did because later I became very unwell and having that extra support saved me.

Dealing with Death

At 20-weeks we took a babymoon to Croatia and spent a lovely week exploring Dubrovnik, Mostar and Kotor. In a market in Dubrovnik an old lady with a stall of knitted items noticed my baby bump and came around to congratulate me. She gifted me some booties for the baby. It was a gesture totally out of the blue, from a stranger who spoke to me not in English, and it floored me. I sat in a nearby church and cried for an hour. I should have had two pairs of booties not just one.

The pregnancy progressed but by 28 weeks I had developed Obstetric Cholestasis (ICP). The hospital wanted to admit me, but I refused. Instead, I stayed at home and was a day patient, every day for almost 8 weeks. If you have not heard of this illness, please look it up. It's horrible and life-threatening for the baby.
https://www.facebook.com/groups/icpsupport/

At 36 weeks it was time to get the baby out as I was extremely ill and the longer, she stayed in the higher risk of her having a heart attack. I was induced, but nothing happened, followed by a C-section. She was taken to special care, and I was traumatised. In the High Dependency Ward, a Consultant Dr looked at her crib and saw the words "Twin A" and asked me, "Where is the other one?" I wanted to punch him.

Thankfully I took my baby home after seven days and, in 2024, we celebrated her 10th birthday. It was the first birthday that I did not mourn the loss of her twin. I reconciled during my healing a few years prior that Twin B sacrificed herself so that her sister could live. It is this thought that has allowed me to let go of guilt and grief and be truly present with my precious child." Krissy Regan

My hope is that in reading these stories you will find some words to help you heal or overcome grief, or to process your own emotions. Despite how much you want to be left alone in your grief sometimes, there are others that need you and you need them too.

Note-worthy tips for Dealing with Death.

- If and when it happens to you remember that you are not alone, there are many people nearby who are dealing with similar circumstances and, while that does not bring back your loved ones, it does mean that many compassionate people exist who could provide a lifeline.
- If you can talk to your partner about pre-emptive topics like money, insurance, wishes, passwords, policies etc. do so.
- Depending on where you live get a handle on what happens with your pension or Superannuation should you or your partner pass. Sometimes you need a death certificate before any funds will be released to you.
- Sadly, there are many expenses associated with death. You may not have access to a few $$$thousand. Who would and could you ask for help in the short term?
- Health and Wellbeing should not be overlooked during death. Doubling down on self-care is one of the best ways to get through it.

Dealing with Death

- Routine is good, but so is some spontaneity and adventure. Embrace this new opportunity to explore or make changes in your life (when you feel ready).
- Honour your loss and your grief, and talk, write, scream and cry. It's good to get it all out.
- Take some duvet days or close the curtains and be alone with yourself if you need to.
- Support groups while cheesy for some do exist for all kinds of scenarios. Social connections will keep you healthy and hopefully help you find joy in continuing with your life.
-

"In a past life, you were a bowl of flour, butter, eggs, sugar, ginger and molasses."

My notes and reflections

Chapter 7
Midlife Masterclass

Do you ever think that hindsight is the best teacher? What would you tell your younger self? If you could coach yourself to cope better with the challenges of mid-life what tools would you employ?

In this chapter I share my favourite mid-life lessons and hope that they help you too. Alternatively, you can write down your own useful experiences and share them with others in your own way and time. Which leads me nicely to lesson number one, Time.

1. Time.

Time Scarcity – Do you ever feel that there is not enough time? Or that you are running out of time? This is called Time Scarcity – a mindset which tells you that time is not on your side.

By mid of life our biological clock maybe telling us time is running out.

Many of us spend most of our lives time dependent. We schedule ourselves seven days a week and we are constantly on the go from one thing to another. We often feel that our life is out of control and there are never enough hours in the day to get everything done.

Of course, this is true and feels unfair. BUT what if our mindset of Time Scarcity is something we can change, and we should seriously consider our relationship with time. Can we find more time in the day, or only give time to the activities that add value to our lives?

Many people I've met admit that they spent too much time at work and not enough time with their children. Most people believe they are too busy to exercise, enjoy hobbies or have a spiritual practise. Many people think that holidays are something to be earned.

Here are three things I recommend helping overcome a mindset of Time Scarcity.

1. Build a "Holiday Moment" into each week. It could be a picnic, a swim, a fun activity, a brunch with friends, a movie night at home, a trip to a nearby town. Punctuating our lives with holiday moments ensures that we don't feel drained and burned out, unable to enjoy downtime. We should not save our holidays for just a few weeks out of 52. If we build in regular "holiday-like" activities, then it would become easier to unwind on a regular basis. We can enjoy spending time with people we love and have regular fun things to look forward to which bring feelings of excitement and joy to balance feelings of stress.

   Several years ago, I trialled a concept called; "Daily Holiday Moments". For one hour each day I did something holiday-like. I listened to nice music; had coffee with a friend; ate a nice meal; or had a bath and a facial. I enjoyed this attitude shift towards holiday hours as opposed to holiday weeks, and it allowed me to be more appreciative for the time spent each day doing something that was both relaxing and joyful.

2. Prioritise your "Musts, Needs and Cans".
Working full-time hours and trying to schedule time for yourself is challenging. The most important thing to consider as you plan your working week is to think of three buckets of time: Can-Do, Need-to-Do, Must-Do. If your week is full of Must Do's than there is little balance in your life, and it is unsustainable. A full day and night of Must-Do keeps us constantly in a state of flight (stress) and puts our nervous system on overdrive.

Take some time on Sunday, or any other day, and think about your upcoming Must-Do and Need-to-Do and then ensure your put some of your Can-Do in there too. A Can-Do is something that is not imperative but would make you feel good. A haircut, a massage, a long chat with a friend, or simply a walk.

If you work shifts, or are chin deep in a big project, your life may be put on hold for periods of time. It can be hard to go back to a less intense routine and slow down to enjoy life again, so it's worthwhile considering how you can factor holiday moments and Can-do activities into your life when the quiet time arrives.

3. Practise "Time Affirmations". A time affirmation is a reminder that time is relative, and procrastination can keep us stuck and unproductive, while working extra-long hours often breeds inefficiency, and wastes time.
Affirmation 1: "There are more than enough hours in the day to do all the things I WANT to do."
Affirmation 2: "Time does not control my life, I choose the things I want to do!"
Affirmation 3: "There is more to life than work and domestic servitude, I value my time and myself."
Affirmation 4: "I don't waste time, and time wasters don't waste me."
Affirmation 5: "I have a healthy relationship with time, and I respect the natural order of life."

Mastering your relationship with time will mean you regain time, have more time for yourself and the things you love, and you will let go of procrastination and time wasters. As you focus on the things you value, and those who value you, you appreciate your time more.

Anxiety is caused by being future-focused and worried about outcomes that may, or may not, happen. Add that to an overscheduled life, and time scarcity, it is no wonder that we have a health crisis.

2. Radical Acceptance.

Radical Acceptance is a state of mind, or being, that enables us to consider all the facts of a situation and then choose to accept what IS, regardless of how painful or unsettling things are.

Our personality type and how we view the world, and the trauma we have experienced will likely determine if we are easy going or more concerned with things we can't control. If you are an empath the concept of radical acceptance will be a challenge.

When faced with the death of a loved one, or seeing a war raging, or innocent people being killed, radical acceptance could feel like a bitter pill to swallow. However, we can choose radical acceptance in situations where the suffering is temporary. A relationship breakdown while heart breaking is temporary, and radical acceptance can help us see the facts, consider the outcomes, and choose to let go quicker.

Losing a job or confronting a stressful life event can become easier when we practice radical acceptance. **Radical acceptance reduces our need to fight, overthink, suffer, ruminate, blame or become bitter.**

Another way to think about radical acceptance is to think of the serenity prayer.

"God grant me the serenity to accept the things I cannot change, Courage to change the things I can, and the Wisdom to know the difference."

Or you could tell yourself.

"There are plenty more fish in the sea."

"There is an abundance of jobs, and this one was not right for me."

"Relationships come and go, and I deserve to be treated well."

"My health and weight may not be ideal right now, but I'm willing to work through this period and be stronger and healthier on the other side."

"I accept that my emotional and mental health is suffering right now, and I will focus on healing my heart and quietening my mind."

"I have no idea how this will work out, but my need to feel safe is more important than my need to please others."

3. Self-love

Self-love is a new-age term for many of us and in most countries the idea of loving yourself is just so icky we can't do it. We are actively taught NOT to love ourselves. We have been conditioned to accept whatever was dished out, and to respect people even if they have abused us.

We only have to look at many examples from the Catholic Church to understand how this has played out over decades. We compromised our self-love and self-respect in order to fit in, be respectable and acceptable to others, and we lost our voices and ourselves in the process.

So, if you have woken up in the mid 2020's and decided it's high time you start loving yourself what could you do to kickstart a new affair with yourself?

The first thing for middle-aged people to do is realise the regardless of their upbringing, and the kind of family they are trying to create, that they deserve to feel whole. Decades of NO self-love will take time and dedication to heal.

You can start to cultivate self-love with three simple actions.

1. Close your eyes, put your hand on your heart and say to yourself, "I love you, thank you for loving me, I love you for loving me."
2. When you look in the mirror do your best Joey Tribbiani from Friends impression, "How you doin'?" Then smile and wink at yourself. "I'm doin' good babe, how you doin?".
3. Close your eyes and think of yourself as a little child between 7-10 years old. Get down on one knee as your

adult self and say to that little child, *"I'm sorry for what you went through; you did not deserve that; I will love you and protect you; you will be OK."*

The longest relationship we will ever have is with ourselves, which is why we should LOVE ourselves. If you need to learn to love yourself, or to let other people love you, the best place to start is with compassion for you and anyone that harmed you. You can, and will learn to validate your own feelings, feel a deeper connection to yourself and others, and develop deeper bonds with your own children as you aspire to be the parent they want to grow old with. Many experts tell us that the best way to be a good parent is to start with parenting yourself.

As corny as you feel (and believe me, I get it), your heart will heal, and your health will improve. It's proven that Oxytocin, the love hormone, can help heal our bodies and repair our cells. So, every time you love yourself you are taking some free medicine.

4. Money

Ken Honda says that you will always lose your first few million. This is the right of passage for millionaires and billionaires. Big money comes with big responsibilities and big risks. From the outside the lifestyle of the rich and famous looks amazing but often they admit to not being happy, whole and fulfilled. Gaining the money was just a goal and once they achieved that goal, they didn't know what to do. They don't feel whole within themselves and making lots of money did not change that.

If you love spending money why not try NOT spending money for a while and use that time instead to give back to your community, volunteer your time, or write a book. The general aim of money is to buy freedom. But freedom is simply "choice". Anyone who has a choice has freedom.

In a time of radically increasing costs, it's a good idea to think about what life you want to live in the next 1-2 years and how much money would make that possible. Remembering too that health is wealth. I think a 1–2-year money lifecycle is good because life is constantly changing, and the needs of our family is always changing. Not to mention macroeconomics and global pandemics are not controlled by the people reading this book.

Money education is valuable for you and your family, as is a healthy appreciation for the geopolitics that drive the modern prices for goods and services. If the spiralling costs of life are freaking you out, it's OK to minimise and economise. The tiny house revolution is growing, the elderly renting rooms to Gen Z is acceptable, as are hybrid cars and solar power. There is no shame in stepping off the money merry-go-round to find a situation that better fits with who you are at any stage of life.

A famous footballer tasked his wife with finding a house in LA when he was relocating from Europe. He asked her to find a furnished house so they didn't have to buy furniture because they would only be there for a year or two. She told him she could not find a furnished house, but she did find a house she liked. He instructed his broker to secure the house and go to IKEA to get furniture. The Broker told the Footballer, *"Rich people don't go to IKEA."* The Footballer replied, *"But smart people do!"*.

As I approached my 48th birthday I decided I wanted to be mortgage free in our primary home, so we decluttered and downsized and we now live in a much smaller home that requires minimal maintenance. I love my smaller house and as a family we actually spend more time together as there are fewer rooms to hide in and we talk more. We still have our own spaces, but we have more time and more money to do the things we love. We can travel more, spend less time cleaning and gardening and save money on bank interest.

I'm quite certain that there are people who think I'm weird for leaving my lovely big house to live in a townhouse before I'm retired but part of the idea was to have a more retired lifestyle in my 40s which allowed me to spend more time with my young family and save for the future. The decision was right for us.

5. Drugs

When I think of mid-life drugs, I'm not referring to the recreational drugs you may have experimented with, or even medicinal cannabis which more people than ever seem to use these days.

As we age and our body starts to slow, creak and groan under the weight of life: things don't always function optimally. This is usually when your medicine cabinet becomes significant, even if it was an area of your home which was largely insignificant previously. Doctors may prescribe drugs for blood pressure, depression, cholesterol, blood thinners, arthritis, HRT or any number of pain-relieving medications. It's common to mindlessly accept these drugs and think we are helping our body.

There is a lot of research and evidence to highlight that those people who choose diet and lifestyle as a drug of choice live longer, healthier and less dependent lives. It is also widely reported that between 2003-2016, fines imposed on large pharmaceutical companies for fraud and other illegal activities amounted to $33 Billion. A new film released in 2024 called, "*FIRST! Do no Pharm*", highlights the influence of too many drugs on our society. Produced by Cereal Killers Movie and staring British Cardiologist Dr Aseem Malhotra, investigates corruption in medical research and the devastating influence of Big Pharma on global health.

We know that wholistic health is good for us, but we accept drugs which are not wholistic. Educational documentaries, podcasts, articles and books are readily available, highlighting how Gut Health; Nutrition; Sunlight; Meditation; Forgiveness;

Wholefoods; Plants and Exercise are the keys to good health and can reverse most health conditions.

A world-leading heart surgeon in the US had to change his profession after realising that his patients could heal themselves without surgery if they changed their diet and took readily available supplements found in supermarkets. His conscience would no longer allow him to operate on patients after he changed the diets of his patients and found their hearts and arteries were healthier just a few short months later.

With so much evidence pointing towards simple foods having the greatest effect on health, as well as happiness, it's a wonder everyone is not following this advice instead of stacking their cupboards, and their bodies full of prescription drugs.

Janette Murray-Wakelin was diagnosed with stage 4 breast cancer in her 60s and decided she would not experiment with modern medicine. She used food instead. Her amazing book, **RAW Can Cure Cancer,** and her inspiring documentary, **Running Out of Time,** chart her run around Australia in 2013 as a +60-year-old woman, running 366 marathons in 366 days to raise awareness of diet, lifestyle and the environment: A Guinness World Record and a life changing example to so many.

I found myself being prescribed more and more drugs in my mid-forties and, after educating myself about health, nutrition, gut microbiome, mental health, sleep and longevity, I decided to give up on drugs and use supplements, herbal tea and fresh food instead. I hope to not go back to prescription medications in the future unless I'm seriously injured in a traumatic event.

It would be nice to see some posters in the GP waiting room which say things like;

- Hey, have you Eaten the Rainbow lately?
- Did you know 75 minutes of Exercise each week prevents most diseases?
- Sunlight is good for you in small doses…..
- Alcohol causes cancer, try Kombucha instead!
- What is the secret to longevity?
  Movement - Homecooked Food - Friendship - Finding your Passion.
- Doctors recommend no more than 1-2 portions of processed meat sandwiches per week to help prevent colon cancer!
- We are sad to tell you that dairy products do damage your heart and calcify your arteries and contribute to Type 2 Diabetes and Alzheimer's. Do take care of your lovely heart and brain!

What health information would you like to see at the doctor's office? Or taught in schools?

6. Relationships

Healthy relationships are 2-sided: "Give and Take".

It's possible you have had many good relationships and many not-so-good relationships by the middle of your life. It's also possible that we have met most of the people we are ever going to meet, and the number of our relationships start to decline. You may even have lost many friends and family due to relationship breakdown or even death.

Healthy, respectful relationships bring feelings of safety and security, and the opposite is true for narcissistic and abusive relationships. Dr Ramani Durvasula is a relationship expert and psychologist who clearly articulates our behaviour patterns relative to the relationships we have in our life. Understanding the role that we have assumed, or has been assigned to us, is helpful in figuring out the traits that make us who we are.

Knowing whether you are the **Family Favourite, the Fixer, the Scapegoat, the Truth-teller or the Black Sheep,** may help you better understand yourself and how you show up for others. It's never too late to unlearn unhelpful behaviour patterns and to distance yourself from abusive people. Our attachment to people who believe they have the right to cause us harm is destructive, and we can, and should, choose to surround ourselves with loving people who want the best for us.

Unfortunately, we may be sent many of the wrong type of people in our life until WE change, and we stop attracting and enabling them.

So, what about Love?

I very rarely hear people discussing Love in all its forms, and falling in love is not the same as universal love. Many people report feeling lonely, unheard, devalued and seeking fulfillment in modern life. I like to think about the hunter-gatherer times on earth when subsistence living, and nomadic life was the norm. Family units stayed together, jewellery was made from simple items found around the place, and people followed the stars and moon for advice on when to go out and when to stay in. Our lifestyle during this time was more in-tune with nature and we didn't need to shop or mass produce things in order to survive. What does this have to do with Love? I think that our world has become so convoluted, complicated, and populated it's hard to feel genuine universal love. And so, we turn to Tinder, Temu, or Amazon!

I experimented with internet dating in my late 20s. It was not for me. I met some very shady people. I was more comfortable with the old fashion way of meeting men, while having far too many drinks at the pub and dancing till dawn. Every manner of trying to find a suitable partner (lover) is laden with risks but our animal instinct means we keep trying regardless of how cringy it is to go hunting for a mate.

Looking for love in mid-life comes with its own challenges, trappings and baggage. It can also be a time for renewal: testing how far we've come in learning how to be a good mate and what partnership feels like. We may better understand our own needs and desires and can help to fulfil someone else's.

How is your relationship with Love?

Do you crave love?

Are you in Love?

Do you feel Loved?

In my 40's I read **_The Five Love Languages_** by Gary Chapman. This book is very helpful if you consider what aspects of Love and Relationships you value.

Prior to having children my Love Cup was filled up by sleeping, eating, sex and having nice holidays with my partner. After having children my love own cup was constantly empty and in order to fill it, I needed to sleep, eat and be alone. The joy of eating an entire meal without being interrupted was something I craved.

Parental love is a different kind of love that tests every ounce of our strength and resilience. Children who feel safe and loved will provide boundless love but may struggle to be detached from you. I remember the first time I left my child for a few days on a business trip, I felt sick the entire time. I had a hole in solar plexus that was aching so much, and I had never felt that before in my life. It is this love that keeps us up at night caring for our children, working hard to provide for them and going to the ends of the earth to make them happy. And then they become teenagers and for some weird reason they can simply fall out of love with us.

We too can fall in and out of love with our own parents. Realising your parents are not the kind of people you aspire to be could come as a difficult revelation for many. People are not perfect; Parents are not perfect and trying to love for the sake of family is the cause of untold trauma. Familial responsibility is a curse that can keep many people trapped in unhappiness for decades.

It's ironic that in modern life while we are not hunting and gathering, we are busy trying to decide what family heirlooms we should hang on to, and who gets the silver spoons.

Whilst loneliness is the quickest way to an early grave should we compromise our own happiness to ensure the parent we no longer like is taken care of? Only you can answer this question, but here is what I've seen all over the world. I've seen some families that love each other without conditions, judgement, abuse and ridicule. I see families that lift each other, encourage each other, and truly want the best for each member of their family. AND then I see those that don't. Or in the words of Anna Karenina, *"All happy families are alike; each unhappy family is unhappy in its own way."*

If you find yourself in the family that perpetuates abuse, ridicule, hate, judgement, conditions, jealousy and resentment then it's probably healthier to choose to detach yourself. You can then focus on your own family and not passing these behaviours on to the next generation. This is self-love and underpins all good relationships.

"I made stew to use up all of our holiday leftovers. The crunchy parts are candy canes."

My notes and reflections

Afterword
Midlife and Then What?

How we navigate midlife will create a foundation for how we unfold as an older person. Strengthening our core (the centre) will help us cope with the highs and lows of the challenges yet to come. We've talked about how our bodies change in midlife and how our youthful, elastic resilience has waned. We need to accept that the same principles apply to relationships, mental health, feeling safe and secure, and being independent for as long as possible.

The two words that I look to for inspiration are, **freedom** and **independence**. I want both for as long as possible.

- Independence is knowing that you have loving people to support you but having agency over where you live and what you can do.
- Freedom is knowing that you can make choices that bring joy to you and others, and that you can make decisions without fear.

When I think of life after midlife several areas of my future come into focus.

- As a parent I want to be needed but not too needy: there is a fine balance.
- I want to be carefree but not careless.
- I want to use money, not let money use me.
- I want to be healthy, active and productive.
- I want freedom and independence to roam but still have a home that doesn't cost the earth to maintain.

Afterword

- I want to experience other cultures and explore places I've never seen and not feel afraid to leave my comfort zone.
- I want to inspire my children to take care of themselves and to follow their hearts.
- I do not want to be a burden to the planet or to other people.
- I don't want to be a moaning, bitter older person.
- I want to do a lot of things.

Many people I admire are working hard and evolving into different versions of themselves in their 60s and this gives me great comfort. When I turn 60 my youngest child will be graduating high school. As she turns into an adult, I will be evolving into the next version of myself and I want to do that with health and vitality, and an open mind and excitement for both of us.

I don't anticipate feeling empty nest syndrome because as soon as my kids want to leave home, I believe I have permission to abandon the nest too and spread my wings. I do joke with my children that I will be backpacking and visiting them wherever they live when they leave home.

The preciousness of life and freedom came sharply into focus in 2020 with the arrival of a global pandemic, followed by unrest and wars in several countries. Protecting our freedom and appreciating life and the irreplaceable value of our natural world reminds us to live in the moment, be at peace with ourselves, and imagine a future that is safe and healthy for everyone.

A book that reminds me of the fragility of the world we live in is called **Cloud Land,** written by Penny Van Oosterzee. She is a phenomenal woman and Professor at James Cook University. She is an award-winning scientist, author and environmentalist. Her book, Cloud Land is one of the most enlightening and frightening books I've ever read because she highlights the evolution of the Australian continent, its people and its animals and plants. Understanding how our country evolved over millions of years and realising that less than 20,000 years ago much of the area I live was shrouded in rainforest and volcanoes is something I reflect on deeply.

I love swimming in a former volcano called Lake Eacham, a crater lake. If you have never heard of it, check it out on Wikipedia. It's also referred to in Penny's book, Cloud Land. Lake Eacham was created approximately 10,000 years ago. What makes this fact so profound to me is that we spend so much time worrying and thinking about menial things when the whole planet can change in the blink of an eye. Our existence here is not a forgone conclusion. So next time you are worrying whether to invest, or not to invest, just remember our world is largely unstable and you can think that all is safe and secure, but you really have no control of what can happen: like a volcano erupting or a tsunami.

Afterword

It is that mindset that reminds me to embrace life, appreciate my natural environment and the abundance of good things we can find for free within arm's reach.

As life speeds up and we rely more on technology which requires electricity, and we also know that the mental health of our younger generations is suffering, it's up to us, slightly older generations, to show them how we can live at a slower, more meaningful pace of life. Understanding that breathing is a gift, choices are a gift, and access to everything we could possibly ever want is beyond decadent.

You may have seen documentaries about the African Tribe who live long and healthy lives without any diseases and who have the healthiest gut bacteria in the world compared to many who live in developed countries. These people have no convenience food, no electricity and no cars. They hunt, gather, share and appreciate their natural environment.

Of course, we can't all run off to Africa and live off-grid, however, what we can learn is that simplicity is the key and overcomplicating our lives continually with more stuff, excess admin and on-demand food is preventing us from living a simple and abundant life doing the things we really enjoy.

I hope that this book has provided you with some ideas to reflect on. That you celebrate your wisdom, and your work, and visualise a future filled with all the things you love. There will be obstacles and grief to overcome, and the world will keep changing, but so can you.

I choose to sleep in a room without blinds and curtains because I want to wake up to natural light every morning: I want the sky to be the first thing I see when I open my eyes. Each morning when I wake up, I try not to open my eyes right away. I lie on my pillow, and I say to myself; thank you for a new day, thank you for a comfortable bed, thank you for a healthy body and a safe place to live. I step out of my bed and appreciate that whatever is in store for me today is going to give me an opportunity to learn new things, and to be different version of the ME I was yesterday. I act compassionately to myself if I made mistakes the day before, and I remind myself that I don't need to be rooted in my past. Today I can be whatever I choose to be.

Every single professional development coach, monk, and self-help guru will tell you the exact same thing.

"Simple, consistent, healthy rituals are the key to a happy and successful life!"

Or in other words – **KISS – Keep It Simple Stupid!**

And with that thought I will say good luck with midlife and beyond. Take care of yourself, be a good person to others, appreciate the natural environment, and choose to spend time with people who value you and value the things you value.

Afterword

Don't be afraid of the next chapter of your life – really you are just getting started. The first half was a warmup. You now have several decades to really make the impact you want, to leave a great legacy, and to be as wonderful as you want to be.

"Grandma says it's important to use the proper fork when you eat in a restaurant. What's a fork?"

My notes and reflections

About the Author

Krissy Regan was born in 1975 in Townsville, Queensland, Australia. She has lived in 7 countries, working and travelling to more than 40. Krissy counts herself lucky to have met and worked with many inspiring people around the world. From riding motorbikes in Vietnam, teaching English in Poland, organising events in Africa and Brazil, Krissy's life lessons stem from spending time in other cultures, having older and younger friends and a continual focus on self-reflection and future growth.  This is Krissy's 6th book, her healthy midlife side-hustle, her passion, and quite likely her purpose in life. Krissy is a mum, marathoner and mentor. You can follow Krissy on Facebook and Instagram. She is known as **The Wellness Poet.**

Her website is: **thewellnesspoet.com**

"At 44, I was not thinking about 49 but at 49, I am thinking about 59! Funny isn't it how a number has more or less significance depending on where we are. Where I am right now is half-way through my life and this is profound, empowering and frightening. I've had a pretty decent first half of my life and I'm really keen to make the second half decent too. So, what could the next 49 years look like? 💡

I'm aware and conscious enough to know that I am largely responsible for my gene expression, my goals, dreams and my well-being. I'm currently not taking any medications except supermarket supplements and largely I'm pain free and quite mobile. I make intentional choices and know how quickly clutter and cholesterol can creep in.

The best anti-aging medicines are fresh food, fresh air, exercise, limiting stress, loving yourself, stretching, meditation and restful sleep. Many of these can be done for free or very cheaply. This is the most valuable lesson I've learned in Midlife. Surgery and face needles are not really my thing. There will always be things we want to improve or accumulate but often this causes us to live in a state of deficit or lack, and we do know that this is not a helpful mindset.

So, what do I imagine for the next 49 years? 🧐

- *I have a decade of schooling to navigate with my children. I want them to be broadminded, kind, inclusive, healthy young people. So, what can I pass on that is helpful to them but not limiting? This is my dilemma to navigate.*

- *I would like to write more books, travel more, and participate in more marathons.*
- *I would like to meet some of the people that have inspired my health journey and continue to learn new things from them.*
- *I want to work with good people, doing good things.*
- *I want to avoid narcissistic, nest-feathering, nepotists. These people are my nemesis and I'm so bored of them at this stage of my life.*
- *I want to continue to declutter, minimise wants and desires, and focus ways to give me more time to do things that bring joy and fulfillment.*
- *I want to age gracefully, (and disgracefully) when the opportunity presents itself.*

I ran alongside a man in the 90-94years age group in the 2024 Sydney Marathon. I also ran alongside women in the 70-75years age group. In these moments my doubts died, and I felt strength from their efforts. Marathon running is not the only way to see the world but it's a cool way to see the world.

At this stage of my life, I realised that I am an "expert" with this midlife stuff, and it is both a blessing, and sometimes a curse. Which prompted the title for this book.

The Blessings and Curse of Midlife by Krissy Regan

This book is not just my experience of midlife. It includes insights, tips, and hard lessons from people all over the world. This book delves into some of midlife's most challenging topics including health, wealth, work, and dealing with death.

This is not a typical "mid-life crisis", old woman whinge, it is an empowering book aimed at both men and women who want to understand this challenging phase of life and feel excited about the future. There is so much to learn about life in the middle stages, and very little collated educational or inspiring resources that are relevant to most people. It's been a joy to research and write this book, and I'm excited to share it with you. 👐

Thank you for being part of my midlife journey. I've got a long way to go, and at the halfway point I've learned a lot of tough lessons and experienced many amazing things. The idea that I will have many more tough lessons could cause anxiety, but with good health, resilience, belief and a safe circle of people to support me I know I will be OK. 👋

So, 49 is feeling pretty good and I am excited to see where the story goes next. My biggest revelation of 2024 was that so far, I've overcome everything!

I've overcome sexual abuse; emotional and mental abuse; workplace bullies; school yard bullies; depression; infertility; IVF; miscarriage; obstetric cholestasis; adrenal fatigue; PTSD, NASH; toxic colleagues, and myself! 😊 🖐

Realising I've overcome everything that has been gifted to me has inspired me to be even stronger." 🫶 Love and Health, Krissy 😊

www.ingramcontent.com/pod-product-compliance
Lightning Source LLC
Chambersburg PA
CBHW062050290426
44109CB00027B/2778